THE ONLINE BOUTIQUE
CEO

HOW TO START AND RUN A SUCCESSFUL ONLINE CLOTHING BOUTIQUE FROM SCRATCH

DENISE FONWEBAN ULASI

~ *Copyright, Disclaimer & Legal* ~

state and local governing professional licensing, business practices, advertising, and all other aspects of business in the specific area is also their sole responsibility.

The Author and Publisher of this guide assume no responsibility or liability whatsoever on the behalf of any Purchaser or Reader of these materials. You may not modify this guide in any way as it is considered copyrighting and legal action will be taken against you.

~ *Dedication* ~

*This book is dedicated to everyone reading the book right
now and either looking to start an online clothing boutique
from scratch, or looking for tips and strategies to help
grow and move their existing online clothing boutique
forward. I hope you enjoy reading this book and find value
in it as much as I've enjoyed writing it.*

Denise.xx

~ *Table of Contents* ~

Part1

GETTING STARTED

Introduction

With so many successful businesses dominating the digital space such as Amazon worth $685 billion (LaMonica, 2018) and Facebook worth $64 billion (Nelson & Karaian, 2018), starting an online business now proves a very lucrative business opportunity. In fact according to Direct Line for Business, there are 8 million people in the UK (even higher in the USA) currently running an online business through buying and selling products online or selling their own created products (Winch, 2013). This growing success in online businesses can also be seen within online clothing boutique stores such as Asos recently reporting revenues of £1.9 billion in 2017 with pre-tax profits of £80 million, and Boohoo recording sales of £294.6 million and profits of £30.9 million (Williams-Grut, 2017). Other successful clothing brands reporting success are Misguided valued at £700 million (Craven, 2017) and Pretty Little thing reporting revenue of 72.7 million (Hamanaka, 2017).

Mintel (2017) recently reported that Brits spent £16.2 billion on online clothing in 2017 resulting in a 17.2% increase within the online clothing market.

However it appears this number is expected to grow even further as PRNewswire (2017) revealed a forecasted growth in the industry by 55.3% in the five years leading to 2022 thereby dominating other sectors as the third fastest growing sector. This therefore signals a booming online clothing industry and therefore an opportunity you can equally profit from.

With so much success online, it is no wonder more and more people are taking advantage of this opportunity and tapping into this digital pie. The appeal and benefits of owning your online e-commerce business versus a traditional brick or mortar store is now even more enticing especially given the fact that with an online business you can reach out to a wider audience, the costs of starting an online boutique are lower than an offline business, the processes can easily be automated, and the business can be operated and run from home or anywhere you chose to.

When I started my online boutique FashVie in 2016, one of my biggest obstacles was finding a manual or at least a guide that could teach me step by step how to start my online boutique from scratch.

Google was swamped with different sources of irrelevant information, with no direct relevance to starting an online clothing boutique.

Of course this made the whole process of starting an online store confusing and overwhelming for me and also resulted in a lot of trial and error, losing out money, investing on the wrong inventory and implementing the wrong business strategies which simply just weren't working. These business struggles are what has essentially inspired the writing of this book "**The Online Boutique CEO**" - a practical and intensive step by step guide to helping anyone start and grow their own successful online clothing boutique from scratch.

This book is based on a combination of my personal experience running my online boutique over the years and business research, with the aim of providing a simple, straight to the point, no fluff, and actionable step by step process to help you start an online based boutique business. It is hoped that this book will be of use to both new and existing clothing businesses in helping them achieve long term business success.

First Things First

So now you have decided that you want to start your own online boutique business. Great Job! Starting your own business can be a very fun and rewarding experience although also challenging and demanding, but overall a profitable experience.

Starting a business in my opinion is like *"having a baby"*. It is exciting, emotional, changes your lifestyle, more responsibility, sleepless nights, and an almost non-existent social life, because you have to spend all day and night nursing that baby, looking after it until it grows into an adult and can function on its own.

Overall it is an exciting, rewarding and profitable experience. After all you are now building your own long term business lineage that could potentially leave an impact in generations to come.

However there is more to starting your own online boutique business than just coming up with an idea and making money out of it or having a burning desire to become your own boss. It will require several sacrifices, consistency and determination.

In fact be prepared to become your own manager, employee, accountant, marketer, sales person, advertiser, etc. especially if you are starting all on your own. Please bear in mind that this is not aimed at discouraging you, but preparing your mindset for the big journey ahead.

Hence given the fact that starting a business requires a lot of commitment and sacrifices, you need to ensure you are mentally and physically prepared for the big journey ahead.

Online VS Brick and Mortar?

So should you start your boutique online or offline?

One of the big questions most people tend to have is deciding on whether to start online or to start a brick and mortar store offline. Now the answer will be dependent on a number of factors listed below;

Finance

Financially it is obviously more expensive to open a brick and mortar or traditional offline boutique. Firstly you need to think about the cost of premises, stationery, inventory, perhaps paying some staff, etc. As you can imagine it could cost you thousands of pounds or dollars to launch such a business. However with an online boutique, you only need to worry about the cost of getting your website up and running, getting some inventory and you are pretty much good to go. Since you are based online, less inventory is required in comparison to a brick and mortar store which usually needs to be fully stocked to appeal to customers.

Customer Reach

With a brick and mortar or offline store, you are only able to reach out to customers in your local and geographical area who pop into your store to shop. However, with an online boutique, you are not only limiting yourself to your city but can reach out to customers worldwide – remember you are on the world wide web. Recently however, there has been an influx of offline boutiques now opening online stores in order to appeal to a wider audience with some reporting more sales online than offline. For example, the UK high street clothing brand "Next" currently sells both online and offline and recently reported an increase in sales due to an online presence by 13.6% despite a fall in offline sales (Cox, 2018).

Flexibility

Another value of starting an online boutique versus an offline one is the flexibility to run that business and make money from it whilst still working on your full time or part time job, studying or focusing on other life commitments. You are not required to make any drastic changes to your lifestyle to operate and run an online boutique. With an offline store however, you need to be physically present in the store to attend to customers and make any money. If you close that business, you don't make any sales (unless of course you are equally trading online).

Tangibility

One reason most people tend to opt for offline stores over online ones is due to the tangibility factor. Some customers' still prefer to see, feel, touch and try on products prior to buying them – something offline stores offer. However with an online boutique, this option is unavailable which can put some people off. Nevertheless with some good product images, video blurbs and detailed item descriptions, most people tend to be ok with shopping online which is still proving a very popular option.

Personally I do not own a brick and mortar offline boutique at the moment as my business is doing pretty well online and I do not see the point of incurring additional expenses offline. Moreover so many offline retail stores are now closing down (*just read the news or look around you*) every single day due to competition from online counterparts which again could indicate a red flag trying to open an offline clothing store.

So in conclusion, I will recommend you start online to test the waters, then once your business picks up or if you have the finances and resources available, you could then also open an offline store. It's really a personal decision and up to you which option resonates best with you. Remember pop up shops and showrooms are also cheaper alternatives to selling your products offline.

Online Boutique Mistakes to Avoid

Now that we have explored some key basic steps to getting your online boutique up and running, here are a few important things you need to be wary of, when starting your online boutique.

Don't be A Shopping Mall

Starting an online boutique gives you the freedom and flexibility to sell as many products as you want online. However the one big mistake you can make is trying to sell everything out there. When I initially started my online boutique Fash Vie, one mistake I made was trying to sell everything - from handbags, clothing, shoes, to hair extensions, etc. Not only did this present a very confusing and conflicting message to my customers about what exactly my brand was about, but it gave my website a rather messy feel, hence putting people off. So instead of trying to be a jack of all trades, find a niche and stick to it. Remember people don't know who you are, especially when just starting out, so don't try to present them with conflicting brand information. As your business expands, you could then start looking into diverting to other options.

Buying Too Much Inventory

Inventory is one of those things that can either make or break your new online store. This is essentially the core to your online boutique success and where most of your money will be tied up on. So when starting out, it is extremely important to not invest too much money on inventory too early on in your business. Remember you are still an extremely new brand and not so many people know about your brand just yet. If you go ahead and invest thousands of dollars on hundreds of units, not only will you need to find space to store all that inventory but you also risk your products not selling and all your money being tied up in stock.

A great way to avoid this is to look into other inventory sourcing strategies such as **Dropshipping** - which involves buying products only after your customers have paid you. This is discussed in more detail later on in this book.

Expecting to Get Rich Overnight

One reason most entrepreneurs and business owners fail is simply because they quit too early on in their business journey. They start a business today and expect to start making money as soon as possible which is simply unrealistic and unattainable in most cases. What you need to focus on initially is creating that brand awareness and building a relationship with your clients as a trusted brand. Once people start to discover your brand and trust you, they are likely to start purchasing from you in the long run.

It might take a day, a week, a month and even years to see any results, but this will all depend on how well you chose to run your business and mostly how consistent and patient you are during that journey. So do not quit your job just yet, keep working on that business and it will eventually pay off.

Making Excuses

One reason most businesses never succeed is simply because of the excuses. I've received so many emails and messages from clients constantly telling me they want to start an online boutique but do not have the money, time, other commitments, etc. What I call this is Excuses!

If the CEO's of successful multi-billion dollar companies made excuses each time they had a business idea, there will be no business out there today. I started my online boutique Fash Vie with less than £200. Yes that's right! I self-taught myself on how to create my own website. It took me weeks and even months of trial and testing but thanks to Google, Youtube and books, I was able to create my first ever ecommerce website. I then decided to use dropshipping as an inventory sourcing approach which also saved me thousands on wholesale inventory. If money is a problem, why not find ways to save money through cutting back on some expenses you don't need, taking some extra shifts at work, or even borrowing from family and friends? Instead of making excuses as to why you can't start your business just yet, why not invest that time finding other ways to work around what you have right now and make the most of it? You see, there really is nothing stopping you from getting started but yourself.

Planning Your Success Strategy

Planning your success strategy is extremely vital when starting your online clothing boutique. Think of your success strategy as a roadmap to your overall business success. Your success strategy comprises three key areas namely; *your mission, your vision and your strategy.*

MISSION

Your mission is the *"core message of your brand"*. What do you want to be known as? What do you want your brand to represent? What do you want people to remember your online boutique as? Start brainstorming on the core message of your online boutique and what you want it to represent and note this down in your worksheet. Remember it doesn't have to be perfect at this stage as you can always revisit this and change as you progress with your business.

VISION

Your vision refers to the long term goals for your business. This is the part where you visualise more long term. Where do you see your brand in the next 3-6 months, 1-3 years, etc? I want you to really get your thinking caps on and start visualising and writing down where you want your brand to be in the next few months and years to come. It may sound crazy and unattainable right now, but that's the whole idea! Just write those crazy thoughts down. You will soon look back and wonder why you ever thought it was a crazy idea.

STRATEGIC OBJECTIVES

Your strategic objectives are basically your plan of action, your to do list, what steps you intend to take to achieve that mission and long term vision. Purchasing this book is already one strategy since you are taking action towards achieving that long term vision of starting your own online boutique.

ACTION PLAN

MY MISSION IS..

MY VISION IS...

MY STRATEGIC OBJECTIVES TO ACHIEVE THESE ARE...

Identifying Your Niche/Target Audience

Now that you have decided to start your own online boutique, one of the most important first steps to starting your online boutique is to identify a niche or market you want to focus on. Overall the best inspirations and motivations should come from things you love and personally enjoy, from personal experience, and most of all something you have a passion for. There are a few areas you could look into such as;

- ☐ Women clothing only
- ☐ Men clothing only
- ☐ Shoes only
- ☐ Lingerie only
- ☐ Handbags only
- ☐ Fashion Jewellery only
- ☐ Hair Products
- ☐ Cosmetics

☐ Beauty Products

To help determine which niche or areas you can focus on, a few questions you could look into to help you decide are;

☐ *What inspired you to want to start your own online boutique?*

☐ *Do you have some fantastic new designs you have that you think people will love?*

☐ *Are you a fashion blogger looking to make more money from your blog?*

☐ *Have you seen other boutiques and thought you could start one better than that?*

☐ *Or maybe you are just passionate about fashion and would love to become your own boss?*

☐ *Do people compliment your shoes all the time? Maybe you could open your own shoe boutique. You would already have some potential clients.*

☐ *Or maybe it's your handbags people love? Again you could start a handbag boutique.*

☐ *Perhaps it's your jewellery people always compliment you on? Why not start your own fashion jewellery boutique.*

- *Do people love your dress sense? Then perhaps think about selling dresses online.*
- *Which type of products from the list above do you tend to spend MOST of your money on, on a weekly, monthly basis? Now that might just be the niche you should focus on. Something you already enjoy doing and have a passion for right?*

Do not try to be broad when selecting a niche by trying to sell everything in your online store because not only will your customers find this confusing, but it will also be difficult for you to identify your target market. **After all, you are not a shopping mall**!

For example when I started Fash Vie, it was just an online boutique selling all sorts of products from women's dresses, tops, jeans, handbags, shoes, waist trainers, hair, etc. The business was just all over the place which made it very difficult for me to sell my products as people stumbling on my website were presented with confusing data. For example, if I came to a website looking for a plus size dress, I would expect to find similar products on the website and not pet clothing or car accessories.

Eventually I learnt from this experience and today, Fash Vie specifically targets the working class or professional woman within the age group of 21 − 45. This makes it easier for me to identify my target audience and therefore invest my time and resources only marketing my brand to those who need it the most.

So don't feel like you are missing out on anything by not selling everything out there in your boutique. Trust me, focusing on a target group will help a great deal with the launching of your online boutique which you will discover later on in this book. Whichever decision you make at this stage will have a long term impact on your overall business strategy so please take your time and brainstorm properly.

So what I need you to do right now is start by jotting down a few niche ideas you have decided to come up with. Take a note of at least 2-3 an and we will proceed to researching the market to ensure that there is a potential demand for your product(s)

ACTION PLAN

THE NICHE IDEAS I HAVE SELECTED ARE:

- ☐
- ☐

- ☐

- ☐

- ☐

- ☐

- ☐

- ☐

Market Research

Now we have some ideas, it's time to undertake some market research to ensure there is a need in the market. Identifying a niche or business idea for your online boutique is amazing. However if nobody is interested in your products or services, then is there really any point in starting that business in the first place? So before we get too excited and carried away, today's plan is to undertake some market research to ensure people are indeed ready for your online boutique business.

Given the excitement that comes with starting a business, most people get so carried away with their idea that they forget to do their homework - **Market Research**. Being passionate about your business idea, doesn't automatically mean people will feel the same way about it.

Think of your business as an examination, and market research the revision required to make it a success. If you go into an examination room unprepared, then unless you have some super genius powers, be prepared to fail.

So How exactly do you do Market Research?

Research can be done in so many different ways. For example, when starting an online boutique business a great tool to find out what products are in high demand for your online boutique is on Amazon.

<u>Amazon</u>

Amazon is probably one of the biggest online e-commerce chains in the world, whereby people go every single day to not only search for products but are willing to spend money on those products too. So what better platform to undertake your research than Amazon?

Assuming your niche or idea is on selling plus size clothing, then ideally you would want to do a search on amazon for **"plus size clothing"**. As you can see Amazon is instantly bringing up some great suggestions of what people are actually searching for around the cat tshirt niche as shown below.

Now these are some niche suggestions you could look into incorporating for your own online boutique. e.g you could look into specialiasing on selling plus size lingerie, maxi dresses, bathing suits, etc.

Another great way to search for best selling products on Amazon is to use the **"<u>Amazon Best Sellers</u>"** tool. So assuming your niche or idea is on selling plus size clothing, then you would want to do a search on amazon bestsellers to find the products that are selling the most thereby indicating high demand as shown below.

This immediately tells you what type of products are hot in demand and what people are willing to spend money on, thereby giving you a good idea on which of these products you too could look into monetizing on. Remember you don't have to sell the exact same products but could look into incorporating similar designs to your brand. Preferably, you should aim for products ranking within the top 100 best selling products.

Check out their reviews, see what the positives are and how you could make yours even better, then see what the negative reviews are and see how you could build upon them to your own advantage.

eBay

Similar to Amazon, you can also undertake product research, via a big ecommerce platform like eBay. The good thing about undertaking research within eBay is the fact that people go there every single day looking for products to buy and **SPEND MONEY ON**. Therefore this should give you a great idea on what types of plus size clothing people are ready to spend on.

So if you visit https://www.ebay.com/ then search for plus size clothing, immediately you would notice some great keyword suggestions of what people are actually searching for and ready to spend on - definitely some great ideas to add to your collection.

Now you can see ebay again immediately starts to suggest the popular keywords that people are looking for. Ebay also shows you the number of products sold which can give you an indication of what products are being sold the most.

Google Keyword Planner

Another great platform to research product ideas and most importantly see if there's a demand out there in the market is to use the **Google Keyword Planner.** The Google keyword planner will help determine if a product keyword has enough search volume and demand to give you a good amount of sales. For example if I do a keyword search on *plus size clothing*, it brings up monthly search volumes of between 100K - 1M searches every single month.

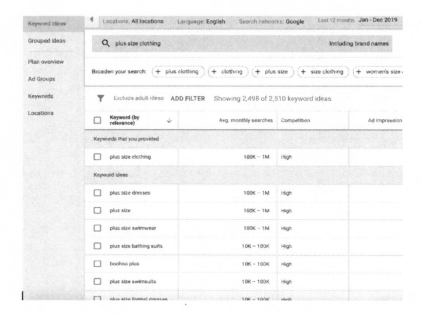

This means 100K - 1M people in the world are going on Google and searching for plus size clothing every single month thereby indicating high demand. It even brings up more suggestions around the plus size niche e.g plus size dresses, plus size swimwear, plus size formal dresses etc thereby giving you even more ideas for your brand.

Other Research Strategies

Similar to Amazon and eBay, you can also undertake product research on ecommerce platforms like Aliexpress. Visit those websites, search for the product in your niche e.g "plus size clothing" and see what type of products are ranking high. You can usually tell this from the number of orders sold on each item. Then use that to get some ideas for your own online store.

Another great way to undertake research for your online boutique is to simply spy on your competitors and see what type of products they are selling, what feedback their customers leaving and how you could use this information to your own advantage - without completely copying your competitors of course.

Other platforms to undertake research for your online boutique include using; **Google Trends** . Google Trends is a great platform to check how frequently a product is being searched for and demanded over the course of a long period of time. It is a great way to establish whether a product is just a seasonal or trendy product, or if it is an evergreen sustainable product.

You can also use social media polls to find out what others think. Visit vendor websites, take their pictures and upload on your Facebook and Instagram pages, then ask your friends, family and existing audience if they will ever consider buying that product. Remember you aren't actually buying these products just yet but simply using their images for research. Gather feedback and responses from them and start building upon that data.

Marketing Mix

Now we have some market research done, it's time to dive deeper into how you plan to execute your online boutique business through looking into the Marketing Mix which comprises of the 4P's, **product, price, place and promotion** as identified by Michael Porter. For service based businesses, this could also include the three other; *people, processes and physical evidence.*

However we will be focusing on the 4P's which are the most relevant to your online boutique business.

Product/Service – A product is an offer that meets a need in the market. This can be a physical object or a service introduced into the market to satisfy the desire or need after purchase and use or consumption. So for your online boutique, *what type of products/niche do you plan on selling?*

Price – The price is the amount of money the consumer will spend in order to acquire the product or service or how you plan to monetise your business. So *how do you plan to price your products and make money from your online boutique?*

Place – The place refers to the place where you plan on selling the products such as; distribution channels, location locations, availability, transport, logistics. *So where do you plan to sell your products? Is it through your own website or an external platform?*

Promotion – This refers to what methods you plan to use to advertise and market your product. This could be through flyer distributions, referrals (word of mouth), social media marketing, newspapers, networking events, etc?

MARKETING MIX ACTION PLAN

So today's plan is to start brainstorming on and creating the 4 P'S for your own online boutique.

Product (s):

Price:

Place:

Promotion:

Part 2

BUSINESS REGISTRATION & LEGAL

Business Name

Now we have an idea and have also conducted some research, the next step is coming up with a business name. At this stage you might want to start thinking about what to call your business. It should be something straight to the point that immediately tells people what it is you do. It should also reflect on who you are especially if selling services.

The business name is the first thing that any potential buyer is going to notice and in this respect is what is likely to draw people's attention and get them curious. You might have the best idea in the world but if people are looking elsewhere because your competitors name 'looks' more attractive then no-one will ever know. Therefore, it's essential that you strike the right tone with your business' name. Get creative; ask people around you what they think of it. Note down a list of different names and pick which one suits you best. Don't make it too long or too short. Keep it memorable and straight to the point! For example if your name is Sandra and you have decided to start your own fashion boutique.

You could call it something like; sandrasboutique, sandraswears, sandrasstore, etc. Or you could come up with something that doesn't have your name linked to it such as; fabboutique.com, plus size boutique etc.

Once you come up with a name, you also want to make sure that the name isn't already registered or trademarked by someone else, the domain name isn't already registered, and it isn't already being used on other social media pages. The last thing you want is your customers landing on other people's businesses or invest on a name that is already taken by someone else.

- You can check that your domain name isn't already registered at: **NameCheap.com**
- You can check that your business name isn't registered at:

https://www.informdirect.co.uk/company-formations/form-company-byshr/

https://beta.companieshouse.gov.uk/company-name-availability

https://www.sec.gov/edgar/searchedgar/companysearch.html

Your Business Structure

Now we have a business name, it is time to start looking into the different business structures. When it comes to selecting a business structure, there are a variety of options you can choose from, all dependent on how you plan to operate.

Sole Proprietorship/Sole Trader – This is the easiest way to register your business and is ideal if you plan to run your business alone. There is less paperwork involved in getting registered, all the profits earned are yours, however you are also liable for any debts - meaning if you took a loan from the bank and your business went bankrupt, then your personal assets could be liable for repossession by the bank. You are also required to register for VAT depending on whether or not your annual sales are expected to reach a threshold of £85,000 (HMRC, 2020).

So if you believe your sales for the first year will be less than £85,000, then there's no need to register for VAT however you still have the option to voluntarily register.

Partnership - This is ideal for a business being run by two people. In a partnership, you and your partner (or partners) personally share responsibility for your business and are both liable for any debts. This includes: any losses your business makes, bills for things you buy for your business, like stock or equipment. Partners share the business's profits, and each partner pays tax on their share. (HMRC, 2018). The VAT rules again are similar to the above.

Private Limited Company or LLC- This is ideal for those who plan on not just running the business themselves but having other shareholders and stakeholders involved. For example if you are thinking about obtaining funding from investors or lenders (who usually require a percentage of your company in return), or plan to hire employees in the future, then it's probably best to register as a limited company.

As a company you can also pay yourself dividends which are usually not taxed. You must appoint people to run the company (called 'directors') and register (or 'incorporate') it with Companies House.

As a director of the company, you can also become an employee. This means that personal income and business income are separate when it comes to paying tax. You will also be required to pay Corporation tax every end of the year and VAT quarterly if you register for it and PAYE if you plan to hire an employee.

As a limited company you are separate from your business, meaning any debts incurred by the business do not directly affect your own personal assets. You can either register your company yourself, or hire an accountant or solicitor to help. It cost £12 as of April 2018, and usually requires more paperwork completion to be fully incorporated.

PLEASE NOTE: *If you are based outside the UK, then check with your relevant local government on the company* *registration process. For US based readers please check with https://www.irs.gov*

Business Registration

Now you are getting close to your big launch, it probably is a good idea to start looking into getting your business registered. You can register your business either as a sole proprietorship, partnership or ltd company. Below are the different platforms you can look into registering with for different countries.

FOR UNITED STATES

SOLE TRADER OR PARTNERSHIP

If you are using your REAL name as your business name, then there is no need to register. However if using a fictitious business name or anything other than your real name as your business name, then you need to file a DBA (Doing Business As) at:

https://www.legalzoom.com/business/business-formation/dba-overview.html

ALL OTHER COMPANY TYPES - If registering as an LLC or Corp, you MUST register your business. More information on getting started can be found at:

https://www.legalzoom.com/business/business-formation/llc-overview.html

FOR UNITED KINGDOM

SOLE TRADER OR PARTNERSHIP

Register as Self Employed, whether using a fictitious name or your REAL name at:

https://www.gov.uk/log-in-file-self-assessment-tax-return/register-if-youre-self-employed

ALL OTHER COMPANY TYPES

If registering as a Ltd or Plc you MUST register your business with Companies House at:

https://www.gov.uk/topic/company-registration-filing/starting-company

FOR OTHER COUNTRIES, PLEASE CONSULT YOUR RELEVANT STATE OR LOCAL GOVERNMENT FOR MORE INFORMATION.

PLEASE NOTE: This information is valid at the time of publication and may be subject to changes moving forward. Always double check with your relevant governmental websites or legal adviser for any latest changes.

Trademarks & Copyright

Trademarking your name is another important aspect of your business. Although it is not a requirement to do this as soon as possible, it is something to definitely look into as you proceed with your business launch. Trademarking your business name gives you full ownership of that name and the legal right to sue anyone who tries to use your business name for whatever purposes.

Once you come up with a name, you also want to make sure that the name isn't already trademarked by someone else to avoid any copyright issues. The last thing you want is to end up in a legal battle with another company for using their business name. You can check with the Intellectual Property Office to ensure that the name isn't already taken. If based in the UK, you can check this at https://www.gov.uk/search-for-trademark

If based in the USA you can check your trademark name at:

https://www.uspto.gov/trademarks-application-process/search-trademark-database#heading-1

It currently costs £170 as of 2019 to register a trademark in the UK and can be done at:

https://www.gov.uk/how-to-register-a-trade-mark.
This process is usually lengthy and sometimes you might need to get a trademark lawyer.

For those based in the USA, please consult the IRS website at https://www.irs.gov as trademark registrations differ with each state. For all other countries, please consult with your relevant governmental boards.

If your business name isn't showing up as trademarked, then you are good to go. However if your business name is registered within any of these platforms, try and tweak it, modify it and search again until it is available.

Getting A Seller's Permit/VAT Number

A seller's permit is also known as a sales tax license, wholesale license, resale license, sales tax certification and retail license. There appears to be a little confusion around obtaining seller's permit and whether or not you need one for your online boutique?

As a rule of thumb, if you plan on buying products wholesale and reselling or, are physically handling products you sell (e.g. through making your own products) then a seller's permit is required. A sellers permit is also required if you plan on charging or collecting sales tax on your products. In the UK this is equivalent to a VAT registration number.

If you plan on dropshipping, then obtaining a seller's permit may be optional especially given the fact that you are not physically buying, reselling and handling any shipment yourself. However do bear in mind that, seller's permits laws tend to differ for each country and state and its best to check with your local state or government to establish what each process involves in more detail.

So essentially, if you plan on buying and reselling, physically handling products or plan on charging sales tax on your products, then a sellers permit or VAT registration number is required by law.

You can check with the IRS (USA) or Gov.uk (UK) to find out more information on registering for a sellers permit and VAT number.

Your EIN Number

An EIN number also refers to an **Employer Identification Number**. This is the terminology commonly used in the United States of America. In the UK this is similar to the **PAYE (Pay as You Earn)** Reference number.

An EIN number is usually required for businesses that plan on hiring and paying staff. So if you are a sole trader working alone with no employee, then an EIN number is usually not required, instead you can use your social security number.

If you plan on registering your business as an LLC or hiring staff, then you can register for an EIN at:

https://www.irs.gov/businesses/small-businesses-self-employed/do-you-need-an-ein

Please note that, sometimes wholesalers may request for an EIN number in addition to a sellers permit before you can buy from them, so endeavour to check this with your wholesalers. The same rule applies to those in the United Kingdom. So if you are a sole trader working alone with no employees, then usually a PAYE Reference is not required. However if you plan on hiring staff, then you can register for a PAYE Reference at:

https://www.gov.uk/register-employer

DISCLAIMER: Always double check with your relevant governmental websites or legal adviser for any latest changes to these rules.

Business Insurance

No matter how successful your business seems, accidents do occur at times we do not expect. Getting business insurance for your online business is optional, but necessary for your own protection and benefit. Business insurance will also depend on the nature of your business as it is a legal requirement for some businesses to have business insurance.

For example, professional indemnity insurance is required if you offer professional services. If working from home, also check that your home insurance policy covers you to work from home. Even if you have a successful business, disaster could strike at any moment and force you to shut your doors. Although it might seem tempting to cut costs by forgoing insurance, it is a good idea to look into a business insurance policy. There are a lot of cheap business insurance policies out there starting from as little as £5 per month. You can visit www.moneysupermarket.com or www.gocompare.com to compare different insurance providers, do your research right, read reviews others have left before purchasing any type of insurance policy.

Part 3

YOUR BUSINESS FINANCES

Financing Your Boutique

Now you are ready to start your online clothing boutique, there are several options you could look into to help with the financing of your new online store. Depending on the inventory sourcing options you chose to go for and how you plan to run your business, you may or may not require any external funding.

As previously mentioned, one of the key benefits of starting an online boutique versus a traditional brick and mortar boutique is the low start-up costs and capital required. However, if you need help financing your business, then there are so many different ways of financing a business including loans, grants, overdrafts, leasing, etc.

PERSONAL FINANCING: The easiest form of funding to procure is your existing money. A large number of business owners secure part of business funding from their wallet. After all, it is one of the common places to begin with the venture. Available options include personal savings, money acquired from credit cards, friends and family, insurance policies and home equity.

CROWDFUNDING: Crowd funding is a superb option for online fundraising. It brings a community of investors, start-ups, entrepreneurs and business together and lets them meet each other to accomplish their objectives. There are many crowdfunding websites available on the internet that let you promote your promising ideas and materialize them in a better way. However, the drawback of these platforms is high transaction costs that can range from 5% to 10% of the total amount raised. Visit http://www.ukcfa.org.uk/, www.gofundme.com for great platforms to get started.

BUSINESS LOANS: If you are looking for a way to acquire sufficient amounts of money to fund your business, small business loans can provide you with the same at comparatively low rate of interest. However, if you make up your mind to go with this option, ensure to seek help from a community lender or credit union rather than nationwide bank since the chances of approval of your application are more with them.

Business Bank Account

Most people tend to use their personal bank accounts for business. But should you really open a business bank account? While it may be tempting to start your new business venture without looking at the need for a bank account dedicated to your business activity, this might not be the smartest of choice. As your business grows and expands, it's extremely important to separate your business finances from your personal, day-to-day living. Not only is this important to keep proper track of your finances and manageable, having a business account where customers can pay you via direct debit, cheques, seems very professional. While many business current accounts available charge you for their services, there are others that waive the charge as long as you pay in more than a certain amount each month. Make sure that you shop around for the best options and you can take advantage of the best deals – don't assume that your personal banking provider will be the smartest choice for business use. And remember if you find it difficult opening a business account, you can always open another personal account but use it for business purposes - except of course it won't come with some of the benefits offered by a business account.

Accounting, Bookkeeping & Taxes

The moment people hear the word accounting or taxes, they start regretting why they even started a business. I know exactly what you are thinking right now; *I hate anything to do with numbers. I can't even afford an accountant, how do you expect me to do this? Do I really need an accountant at this stage?*

Now this is an area I'm really passionate about because my first ever business was a bookkeeping business. During that time, I encountered different types of clients, from the ones who wrote their finances on pen and paper and the ones who didn't even keep their receipts, invoices etc.

The message here is, do not wait until your business starts making sales before you start keeping track of your books. The little expenses you have already spent on such as; web design, web hosting, domain name, laptop, company registration fees, business insurance, inventory and all those little spends are already business expenses you should be keeping track of.

Now some of you might be lucky to have family, friends that can do your accounts for you, however for others this may not be the case. If you are looking for an easy and affordable way to keep track of your day to day finances, then you can save yourself the costs by using Ms Excel Bookkeeping spreadsheets such as those offered by No Hassle Accounting.

To manage your day to day bookkeeping, you can get this affordable bookkeeping software at: www.nohassleaccounting.com, or alternatively hire a bookkeeper if you can afford to.

You can then hire an accountant *(if required)* for the more complicated tasks such as year-end tax returns and company accounts especially if you run a Ltd Company.

PLEASE NOTE: This bookkeeping software comes free with our **Run Boutique Business Starter Kit.**

Paying Yourself As A Boutique Owner

Before you begin paying yourself a salary from your business, you need to ensure that your business is making a substantial amount of profit (**not revenue**). Do not confuse profit for revenue. Profit is what is left over after all expenses have been deducted and cleared. Revenue on the other hand comes from sales you have received from your customers prior to any deductions.

For example say you are selling a dress for $35 and a customer buys that dress at $35, then $35 essentially is your revenue or sales. For each item you sell, there are a few direct costs that come from the acquisition, packaging and shipping of that product which all need to be deducted from this revenue before you can boast of a profit.

Say for example the cost of that dress was $7, then PayPal or Stripe deducted fees of $2, you then needed to package and ship that product to your customers which also includes the cost of stationery (business cards, flyers, and printing costs), etc.

Now these are your direct costs which need to be deducted from your revenue to obtain a profit. So say your total expenses were $12, then your **profit will be $23** ($35 - $12). You can then only pay yourself from this $23 profit leftover and NOT the $35.

When just starting out your online boutique business, it is usually a good idea to avoid paying yourself too soon, but rather reinvest your profits back into your business until it gains stability. Once your business starts consistently generating profits that are equivalent to 1.5 – 2 times the cost of your living expenses, you can then start paying yourself. For example, if you need $1000 to survive each month, then you might want to wait till your business is generating profits between $1500 - $2000. So calculate your cost of living each month, then multiply that by 1.5 or 2.

If your business is generating that final amount in **PROFIT**, then you could start thinking about paying yourself a monthly salary. Your monthly salary should equal your living expenses, and the rest of the money put back into your business. Remember you can always pay yourself an additional bonus if business is moving even better than anticipated.

So in conclusion, only pay yourself once a business is generating a profit of at least 1.5 - 2 times your living expenses, then only pay yourself the equivalent of what you spend or need to survive each month.

Here's a little summary;

If Business profits for the month = $1500 - $2000

And Your Living Expenses = $1000

You Should Pay Yourself Living Expenses = $1000

Then Put back in Business = $500 - $1000

Part 4

SOURCING INVENTORY & WHOLESALE SUPPLIERS

Sourcing Inventory

One of the most important resources of a boutique is deciding on how to source inventory or what products to sell on your online store. There are three key ways to source inventory for your online clothing boutique.

BUY WHOLESALE

This is a very popular way of sourcing products which usually involves buying products in bulk at a low price from a supplier, then reselling it at a higher price to your customers. You are responsible for all the inventory management, packaging, shipping, branding, etc. This is usually pretty expensive especially considering how much stock you need to purchase in advance and upfront financial commitments.

DROPSHIPPING

This involves selling products on your website with no need to purchase any inventory in advance. Simply find a drop shipping supplier, start selling their products on your website (at a higher retail price), when a customer buys from you, you pass their shipping details to the supplier (keeping the profit) and the supplier deals with the packaging and shipping of products directly to them (more on this is discussed later).

CREATING YOUR OWN PRODUCTS

This usually involves hand making or factory manufacturing your own products from scratch. This could involve either doing it yourself using a sewing machine or sub-contracting the task to third parties to do it for you.

In the next sections however we will be focusing more in-depth on sourcing products through wholesale and dropshipping.

Where to Buy Wholesale Inventory (PLUS Bonus Vendor List)

Wholesale involves buying products at a low cost from wholesale suppliers, and then reselling them at a higher mark-up price to your customers. This is a great option for those who have capital to invest upfront on inventory. However be aware that most wholesale suppliers expect you to buy products in bulk which could be extremely costly.

Wholesale products can either be sourced locally or internationally. Sourcing internationally usually tends to be cheaper for certain products whilst sourcing locally works out best for bulky items. However, where you source your inventory will vastly depend on what type of products you plan on selling. For example, if you plan to sell less bulky items, it might work out cheaper buying internationally since the cost of imports tend to be lower.

If selling bulky or heavier products, then probably best to look into sourcing locally. Although sourcing locally will save you time, some risks and the cost of importing products from overseas, it may also be a more expensive option. All in all, it is best to check what the best options and costs of sourcing locally versus internationally are for you, before you decide on a supplier.

In-order to purchase wholesale inventory, most vendors require that you have your business registered, have a sellers permit or VAT Number to prove your business is legitimate and sometimes have an EIN Number set up too.

Some great platforms you could look into for wholesale suppliers and vendors are;

www.sellpire.com

www.fashiongo.net

www.orangeshine.com

www.alibaba.com

Salehoo

Worldwide Brands

Another great way to find wholesale vendors is to either attend trade shows around your local area which can be found by a quick Google search. e.g If based in London, you can google "trade shows in London" etc.

You can also find wholesale vendors through doing a Google search on your country, plus your respective niche .e.g. if you are based in the USA and selling clothing, then you could google "**clothing wholesale suppliers in the USA**" and a number of options should appear.

A BONUS list of some other wholesale clothing vendors can be found below;

Wholesale Fashion Square

Mikaree wholesale

https://alibaba.com/

https://www.trendsgal.com

https://www.ktoousa.com

https://www.rosewholesale.com

http://www.dearlover.net

https://www.girlmerry.com

https://www.gitiwholesale.com

Zenana Wholesale

http://www.only-lover.com

Yelete Wholesale

https://www.capellausa.com

https://www.emmacloth.com

https://heracollection.com

http://trendystylewholesale.com

Matterhorn Wholesale

Catwalk Wholesale

https://bloomwholesale.com

https://www.fashiongo.net

http://wholesalefashionyetts.com

https://www.blvapparel.com

https://www.lashowroom.com/

https://www.ccwholesaleclothing.com

https://www.nywholesale.com

Dropshipping

For those who aren't familiar with the term, drop shipping is a technique in which the retailer (you) does not keep goods in stock, but instead transfers customer orders and shipment details to either the manufacturer or a supplier, who then ships the goods directly to the customer. With dropshipping you do not need to handle any inventory whatsoever and hence no need to buy stock in advance. Is like selling stock you don't even own. That's how dropshipping works.

In retail businesses, the majority of retailers make their profit on the difference between the wholesale and retail price but some retailers earn an agreed percentage of the sales in commission, paid by the wholesaler to the retailer. With dropshipping you sell a product on behalf of the wholesaler, send the customer information to the wholesaler who then distributes the product directly to the customer while you keep the profits. So you are like the bridge between the supplier and customer.

If you are interested in starting an online boutique, but don't have a lot of money to invest in wholesale stock in advance, then dropshipping is the answer. Other benefits of sourcing products through dropshipping include;

The start-up costs are small: In order to set up a traditional offline boutique, a good chunk of capital is usually required to buy your inventory of products that you wish to sell from your shop. This is most commonly guess work, there's no saying how much stock you'll sell for that month/year so this eliminates having to risk your money in unsold stock.

You can offer items almost instantly: Usually when a retailer wants to start selling a product, they'll have to wait until all of their stock has been shipped prior to selling them on their website. Using drop shipping means that when you decide you want a product on your site, you can start advertising and selling almost immediately.

You can offer a wider range of products: Having the ability to offer a wider range of products is always something a company can aspire to and with drop shipping, it's possible. You don't have to worry about different colours or sizes and where they're all going to be stored, you simply list them on your site and you supplier can deal with the rest.

Testing new products without a risk: When adding new products to your range, the risk of not selling is always an underlying risk. Having to guess what your customers want to buy is a tricky feat for anyone, so being able to test the water without making any true investment is always an advantage for your site.

Time saving is key: Organising your stock and preparing it for delivery can often be a time-consuming nightmare. Using a third party to ship items saves handling, labelling, packing, shipping etc, leaving you time to focus on growing your business in different areas.

How Dropshipping Works

So assuming you are interested in selling clothing for example but have no money to purchase stock beforehand then drop shipping these is the perfect solution. Here's an example on how it works;

1. You find a wholesaler who sells clothing you are interested in.
2. Find out if they offer dropshipping services.
3. The dress is currently being sold at $10.00 on the wholesaler's website; however the retail price in the market is about $35.
4. You then copy the product details and description from the wholesalers' website and paste on your own website.
5. Set it at a higher retail price of say $35 plus shipping costs similar to that of wholesaler
6. A customer visits your website and purchases the dress from you and the money goes straight into your bank account.
7. You then go back to the wholesalers' site and place an order but this time using the customers' details

as the shipping address, and only paying for the wholesale price of $10.

8. The wholesaler then ships dress directly to your customer whilst you gain a profit of $25. So your job is essentially to promote these products on your own website and pass your customers' details to the supplier after they purchase from you.

Imagine you sell about 10 of this single product in one week, then you have just made yourself $250 (25 X 10) for one product in a week. That's an extra $1000 per month for just one product. And guess what, you did not have to risk any money buying inventory, handling any stock or delivery. All you did was send customers to a wholesaler who handled all the hard work.

Ok now think of all the different products you could be selling and do the same calculations and see just how much you can make. The earnings are endless. It's just up to you how many products you will love to sell and how much money you want to make.

A great dropshipping platform to look into for an all in one solution is Dropship Finds. Dropship finds offers you a

FREE web design service where your online store gets designed for you, you receive training on running your business and access to dropshipping suppliers all-inclusive in the membership.

So I will highly recommend you look into that option to save yourself the time and money if you are seriously considering dropshipping. Of course one of the biggest problems with dropshipping is not having physical access to your products, which can get you questioning the quality of the products your customers are receiving.

A great way to get around this is order some samples for yourself first, try them and test the quality yourself. And if they pass the test, you can start selling these on your website too.

How Much Inventory Do You Need?

There is no set in stone amount of inventory required for a successful online boutique. However as a rule of thumb and based on what has worked for me, I will recommend that you have at least 20-30 different products for an average clothing website. These figures of course could be less or more, depending on your online store type.

For these 20-30 products, it is advisable to have at least 2 units of each piece in each size. E.g. assuming you are selling a Bodycon dress, then you want to have 2 pieces each in a Small, Medium and Large **(6 total)**. If selling plus size clothing for example, you could look into Medium, Large, X-large, etc.

The problem however is, most wholesale suppliers expect you to buy a minimum of hundreds of units per piece in bulk. However there are still a few wholesalers out there who offer smaller bulk orders. Do not be scared to communicate with and strike a deal with your suppliers for smaller bulk orders - I've personally done this before with some of my vendors who had no issues selling smaller bulk orders. If you are working with dropshipping suppliers, this usually tends to be easier especially given the fact that, they tend to sell individual units rather than in bulk thereby making it easier for you to order samples in the quantities that suit you with no bulk minimum requirements.

Inventory Management

Inventory management is defined as the branch of business management concerned with planning and controlling inventories. The role of inventory management is to maintain the desired stock level of specific products or items (Toomey, 2012).

Inventory management is another vital part of running your new online boutique and something you will need to do on an ongoing basis. Inventory management can help you with keeping accurate track and control of your stock.

Most website dashboards out there already have systems in place that allow you to manage and control stock, however these functionalities are limited and you may require a separate software to keep accurate track of your inventory.

A great software to look into for managing inventory is **Shopventory** which comes with different prices from $39 per month. They also have a free package which comes with a few restrictions. However, if you are looking for a more cost effective inventory management template to maintain your stock, then I recommend the **No Hassle Accounting** inventory template which only comes at a **one off fee of £29.99**.

This is an Excel based inventory management program which I personally use to keep track of my inventory at FashVie and has always worked a treat over the years.

PLEASE NOTE: This software is included FREE in our **Run Boutique Business Starter Ki**t.

Part 5

YOUR ONLINE BOUTIQUE WEBSITE

Why You Need A Website

Inorder to create a professional and well trusted brand, it is highly recommended that you get yourself a website. After all you are running an online based store so what better place to sell your products than on your own website.

A business without a website should be prepared to lose out on over 95% of its customers. Nowadays, people go on the internet 24/7 searching for all types of information. With technology practically taking over the world, it is vital that you have a business website.

Without the internet, there is no way you would have stumbled on this book in the first place. So you can imagine how many customers you could lose if you don't have a website for your tshirt business.

Secondly owning a website will save you so much time, money and energy in your day to day activities. Gone are the days where you had to open 100 stores in 100 different cities, just to appeal to customers worldwide. With a website, your laptop and access to the internet, you are on the "World Wide Web" and customers can access and purchase your products from just that one little website.

To get your business up and running you will need 2 key things; **a domain name** & **a hosting platform**.

Your Domain Name

Your domain name is the URL name of your business. It is best to name your domain after your business name. So assuming your business name is plus size boutique then your domain name could be something in the lines of www.plusizeboutique.com or co.uk, .net, etc. basically what name best suits you.

You can get a domain name registered for less than $10 per year from **Namecheap**. However if you have another domain provider in mind, you can still use them. If you want to focus on for example UK based customers only, then you could look into a .co.uk domain name.

Although a .com name is highly recommended as this is great especially for attracting a global audience.

If your particular domain name isn't available, you should usually get a few suggestions on different names you could use. Make sure you choose a good and catchy name and remember not to make it too long. If your domain name is too long, people will lose patience trying to type it all out in their browsers and could even misspell it.

So come up with something short, sweet and easy to remember. Once you purchase your domain name, this should usually be LIVE instantly and available for a year.

Web Hosting

Once your domain name is registered, you need to think about some web hosting options in-order to start creating your website. A domain name without a host is like building a house without a roof.

There are several platforms out there which you can use to host your website. However, below are a few I will recommend. One of the best platforms to look into when setting up your boutique website is **Shopify. Shopify** is not only great for ecommerce online stores, but is also very beginner and user friendly. **Shopify** starts at **$29** per month with a 14 Day FREE trial giving you the opportunity to try them out before you make a purchase decision. You can get started with Shopify by **CLICKING HERE..** You can even checkout free youtube videos on *"How To Create a Shopify Store"*.

Shopify also has so many training tools and a fantastic team that can help you with designing your website, so you can be rest assured that your website will be up and running in no time. You can find out more about designing your Shopify store at:

Payment Processors

To sell online, you will need a payment processor that allows customers to pay you instantly. When setting up your ecommerce website, there are a few payment options you could look into to ensure your customers can quickly and easily pay for their transactions online. A few recommended payment processors that are great for your online store are;

PayPal: This is one of the best and safest payment processors to use. It is FREE to register for an account, you can link it your bank account to your PayPal account easily and then transfer any funds directly into your bank account when ready. You can also pay for transactions online quickly using your PayPal account instead of having to key in your bank details all the time.

You can register for a FREE Business Account with PayPal at www.paypal.com. PayPal charges you a small percentage of 3.4% and **20p ($0.30)** on every payment made into your PayPal account. However this isn't substantial considering your transactions are safe and secure.

Stripe: Similar to PayPal is another payment processor known as "Stripe". Stripe is equally great for collecting and processing online transactions directly from your website. All funds paid into your stripe account however are only automatically cleared and deposited directly into your bank account after 7 days. This means unlike PayPal, you cannot instantly deposit money into your bank account as and when you please, but rather have to wait for their timelines for payments to automatically clear. Stripe is great in that it allows customers to pay you quickly via your website using their debit or credit card details with no requirement to register for an account prior to payment, as with the case of PayPal. Stripe also charges a transaction fee of 1.4% + 20p for all European cards and **2.9%** for all non-European cards.

Of course there are many more payment processors you could look into such as **Square**, which is great for accepting all major credit cards and allows you to collect offline payments.

Important Website Pages

When setting up your ecommerce website, there are a few key pages that are essential you have on your website to make information easily accessible to your website visitors and make their browsing experience as smooth and easy as possible. The last thing you want is a website set up with too many irrelevant pages that could confuse your customers and send them to your competitor websites.

Home: Your homepage is the first page customers will see when they first visit your website. So it is essential that the information on your homepage immediately tells customers what your niche is, and what type of products you are selling. So if you are selling plus size dresses, then ideally you should have some of your plus size products displayed on your homepage.

Be clear on what your brand represents and if possible have a welcome message on your homepage summarising what you do, but try not to have too much jargon on that first page as it could send people away. After all, you are running an ecommerce website and not a blog, so less content and more products.

About Us: This is another great page to have so your customers can get a little personal and easily find out more about your brand and what it stands for. Remember when people stumble upon your website, they don't know who you are, where you are based, etc. Hence an about us page builds that trust with customers. It is also a great page to outline your vision, mission and values as a brand.

Product Page: Your website is an ecommerce store which sells products, hence it is important to have a product page or Shop page where people can quickly and easily browse for the products they are interested in.

Shipping & Delivery: Another vital part of an online store is making it clear to your customers how long shipping will take as this will greatly influence their buying decision. Therefore having a page with clear information on shipping times is extremely useful to have on your online store. This will save you a lot of headaches in the future too.

Also make sure your shipping times align with those offered by your dropshipping supplier to avoid any confusion.

Contact Us: Another vital part of an online store is having a contact page with your contact details where customers can easily reach out to you and communicate in case of any problems or in case they need more information.

Refund Policy: Having a refund policy on your website is another great way to clarify your processes to your customers and avoid any future disappointments. Whether you offer a 14 day, 28 day or no refund policy, remember to make this clear on your website so customers are aware of it prior to purchasing.

Shopping Cart: Pages such as My Account, Cart and Checkout are also extremely useful to have on your website Menu. This means customers can easily navigate between browsing products, adding them to their carts and checking out without any difficulties.

Other useful pages to have on your website include, **Terms & Conditions and Privacy Policy pages**.

Pricing Your Products

Pricing refers to how much you charge for your products and/or services. How much you price your products will usually depend on the market, your brand, competition, target audience and other factors. Assuming you want to sell a Bodycon dress at $47, it will be wise to first of all see what competitors are pricing for a similar product in order to determine the right price point. You do not want to end up too cheap or too expensive as you could end up making so many sales but no profits to boast of (if too cheap), or no sales at all (if too expensive).

So try and find the right fit in alignment with your market and industry. As a rule of thumb, you should be able to make at least a minimum of double and a half (2.5) the wholesale price (what you paid for the product). For example, if you purchased a Bodycon dress from your supplier for $7 cost price, then you want to charge at-least $17.5 ($7 X 2.5) and above for that product. Remember you have to take into account the cost of other expenses such as packaging, shipping, etc so you don't end up under cutting yourself. Such a simple pricing strategy will work well for mass produced type products which are bought in bulk and readily available in the market.

Premium pricing is another great approach which works best for certain products. For example, products which are in high demand but not vastly available in the market, very high quality products, products which are handmade or custom made products, or locally produced products. Bear in mind that some people are happy to pay $30 more on a product knowing that it was made in the USA (or locally) as this is usually associated with better or premium quality, whilst others will pay a little extra for products that are scarce and rare to find anywhere else and custom made products.

Finally, pricing will depend vastly on your brand, its mission, its vision, the type of products you plan to sell and how you intend to source them. So make sure you research market prices, plan your pricing strategy prior to purchasing any wholesale products so you don't end up at a financial loss.

Handling Shipping

Another vital part of selling products online is making it clear to your customers how long shipping will take as this is likely to greatly influence their buying decision. If dropshipping, make sure your shipping rates and times mirror those of your suppliers so you do not end up capping down on your profits.

So if your dropshipping supplier is offering a shipping fee of $4.99, make sure this is the same shipping rate on your website or at least incorporated within your price. You can also offer FREE shipping, through incorporating the cost of shipping in your actual products price. For example, if selling a dress for $25 with a shipping cost of $4.99, then you could price the tshirt at $29.99 plus free shipping.

If you plan on buying wholesale and reselling, then you can calculate how much it will cost you to package and post the order out to your customers. You can also offer FREE shipping, through incorporating the cost of shipping in your actual products price. For example, if selling a dress for $35 with a shipping cost of $4.99, then you could charge the dress at $39.99 plus free shipping.

This is a great way to entice customers to buy your products as some people are automatically drawn to free shipping. In doing so, you still get to keep your profits. Try not to make your shipping costs too high or shipping times too slow as this could put your customers off.

Remember you do not have to physically fulfil any orders in real life if dropshipping **(and your customers don't need to know it)** but because your customers are buying from you and not directly from your supplier, they still need to be made aware of shipping times and policies.

Try not to make your shipping costs too high or shipping times too slow as this could put your customers off. Great platforms you could use for your shipping include **https://www.parcel2go.com** to or **Shipstation**.

Part 6

BRANDING & PACKAGING

Your Business Logo

A Logo is extremely vital in building your image and key to branding your business. Your Logo will make you appear a lot more professional, bigger and more established to your audience. This is what differentiates you from competitors and helps you stand out from the crowd.

When you combine a brand with a business name and a logo you have three of the most powerful marketing pieces of a business. When a customer, employee, vendor, lender sees either one of them and they recognize it, you evoke an emotional response, be it good or bad. Deciding on a business logo may not be a quick process. Additionally, you may welcome professional help. My suggestion is to not rush into this piece if you don't have the time or can't find exactly what you want (Rogerson, 2011).

Although having so many different colours to make your logo stand out could sound tempting, it could also end up looking tacky.

Simplicity is key when it comes to designing a logo and it is strongly recommended that you hire a professional to help you decide on the best way to design your logo.

You can get a logo created yourself for free on platforms like **Canva.com**. However if you are not so good at design, it is highly recommended to get a professional to do it for you on platforms such as www.fiverr.com and www.upwork.com

Alternatively you can checkout our LOGO design services at the Run Boutique Academy at:

https://runboutique.com/logo-design/

Business Cards & Flyers

Another powerful way of branding your business and letting people know about your online boutique is using business cards and flyers. Your business cards and flyers will normally contain all your business information including your company name, address, website, email, social media info, phone number and all they need in-order to locate you.

Business cards and flyers can also help to enhance the personal image of a business person. Production and printing costs of business cards are low, they are extremely portable and benefits are high, as they make a statement in the business world. As a result, the market value of business cards is high.

The information on your business cards and flyers should reflect the nature of your business so that people do not have to guess what it is that the card is for or what business it represents.

You may like the idea of a very stylish logo and simple design, but you want to be sure that anyone who looks at your business card knows why they would be contacting your business.

You should always have especially your business cards handy at all times and make sure that when you strike up a conversation with anyone that you hand them your business card and/or flyers. A great place to get your business cards done cheaply and professionally is at www.vistaprint.co.uk or www.vistaprint.com. So get yourself a business card and distribute them to as many places and people as you possibly can.

Branding Photography

Taking pictures of products for your website is another vital part of branding and advertising. You have a few options when it comes to branding photography for your online boutique.

HIRE A PHOTOGRAPHER & MODEL

You can either model your merchandise yourself or get a model to wear your products. Easiest way to get some inventory for your photoshoots is to first of all order a few samples from your supplier (especially if doing drop shipping) in either your size of your models size. You will then need to hire a professional photographer to take these pictures for you. However do bear in mind that this option is very expensive, especially given the fact that most photographers charge per number of pictures, but can be worth the investment in the long run. Another alternative to using models is to lay the products on a flat surface or use boutique mannequins then take the pictures yourself.

TAKE THE PICTURES YOURSELF

You could also save costs by using friends and family to model for you or hire a volunteer model looking to build their modelling portfolio to do it for you at no extra charge. Alternatively, if you are good at photography, then you can also do so yourself or reach out to photography students looking to build their portfolio to work with.

For my online hair brand Yes Weave for example, I actually got my lovely little sister to model the hair for me whilst I took the pictures. I invested in some backdrop, camera, lighting, then she did her own make up, we got a few hair bundles sewn into wigs and she modelled them all, and I finally edited the pictures and posted them on the website. These pictures have worked perfectly well in marketing the hair brand over the years and still do. However our team are now looking into upgrading into more professional shoots sometime by the end of this year. But this could definitely be a great start for your online store.

USE SUPPLIERS PICTURES

Another easier option is to start by using your suppliers' images. This works well if you plan on drop shipping as you will usually have that automatic permission anyway. For those buying wholesale, you will need to seek permission from your suppliers to use their pictures. The risk of course with this is the fact that other online boutique owners might have similar pictures on their websites too but it all comes down to how you market and brand your business.

USING INFLUENCERS IMAGES

When I launched FashVie back in 2016, I worked with a few influencers for a couple of months to get the word out there. What I did was send them out products for FREE, they then took pictures and posted on their social media platforms and next I then reposted their images on my website, social media pages, etc. This was a great way to create that initial buzz for my brand and really worked a treat in getting those first few clients. And most of all I got to use their pictures under the products on my website.

So this is another powerful way to get people wearing your products and using their images on your website to sell your products. This option is also great for marketing but might be an expensive option if you have to use influencers for every single product on your website given the fact that you need to send out so many free products, etc. Nevertheless it is worth a try!

Packaging & Shipping Essentials

Similar to your logo, packaging plays a key role when it comes to branding your business. It acts as a visual representation of your brand and what your customers will see when they purchase your products, and how they will identify and remember you.

Packaging design is the connection of form, structure, materials, colour, imagery, typography and regulatory information with ancillary design elements to make a product suitable for marketing (Klimchuk & Krasovec, 2013).

Packaging is very essential when buying wholesale and reselling products on your own online store, or hand making your own products. With dropshipping, the suppliers deal with the packaging and shipping, however if you are keen on packaging products with your own information, then you can either send your packaging to your suppliers to use on your customer products *(if they offer this service)* or get them to send products out to you first, and then you re-package and ship out to your customers yourself. This usually works a treat, however be wary that it might be slightly more costly for you especially given the fact that, you will need to pay for additional shipping to finally get the products out to the customers.

Some packaging and shipping must have essentials are highlighted next:

Label Printer

You can get it from Amazon or EBay

3 IN 1 Epson Printer

You can get it from Amazon or EBay

Invoice Template

FREE at: https://www.invoicesimple.com

Flyers, Business Cards & Thank you Cards

https://www.vistaprint.com/

Clothing Labels, Label Stickers & Tags

http://zazzle.com

https://wunderlabel.com,

https://www.etsy.com

Poly Mailers

You can purchase these on EBay or Amazon

Shipping Scales

You can purchase these on EBay or Amazon

Clothes Rack & Hangers

You can get these from most stationery stores or from Amazon.

Part 7

MARKETING & ADVERTISING

Wear Your Brand

There is no better way to promote your new online store than wearing your brand or showcasing your products in real life. This is a great marketing strategy for promoting and advertising your online store. The truth is, people are ten times more likely to buy from you if you personally use the products you sell. After all, why should they trust buying the product from you if they've never seen you use that product before? This is not to say you should use or wear or use every single product you sell in your store, but if you can carry at least a piece of your brand with you in some form, this could be extremely beneficial to your business.

Wearing your brand is a pull marketing strategy in that it pulls customers to you rather than you constantly pushing products out to their faces. Now assuming you have an online store selling women's clothing, and then decide to wear one of your dresses for an event. Whilst at the event, someone suddenly walks to you and compliments your dress, asking you where you got it from?

You can then refer them to your website, hand them your business card to go purchase theirs too. Now you've just won yourself a customer who was pulled to your product through you merely wearing your brand - and this happened with no extra marketing effort. Imagine if 3 other people fell in love with your dress, that's even more money in your pocket. So always find a way to wear or try and incorporate your brand everywhere you go with you!

Not only is this marketing method free, but it is extremely powerful and can result in powerful sales conversions.

Use Social Media Influencers

In this new digital era, collaborating with social media influencers is now becoming a part of every company's digital marketing strategy. Social media influencers are typically people with a huge social media following or fans, be it on Facebook, Instagram, Youtube etc. Think of them as social media celebrities! Because influencers already have a large following of fans who trust them, companies benefit greatly from working with them through getting quick and fast exposure. The goal however is to work with influencers who are relevant to your niche.

So assuming that you have an online clothing store targeting plus size women, then ideally you want to work with plus size influencers since they are most relevant to your niche. If your niche is fitness, you want to work with health and fitness influencers, etc.

To get started working with influencers around your niche, you can visit popular social media platforms such as Instagram.

If using instagram, do a search on: #plussizeblogger #plussizemodel #plussizeinfluencer etc or other keywords around your niche. This should bring up different images.

Click on the images, then visit the relevant pages to see how popular they are and what engagement their profile is getting through comments, likes and views. Pay close attention to the type of comments being left under their pictures. You don't want comments that only mention an emoji or one word statements like *"cute", "nice",* etc.

You want to make sure people are really curious to know where they got those products from, or asking some form of questions about the product being promoted, the brands etc.

Another great way to find influencers is to spy on what type of influencers and brand ambassadors your competitors are using. Then see if you can also do business with them.

Next check their instagram bio to see what they do and how you can get in touch with them. You can also check to see if they already promote other brands on their page and this will give you a good indication on whether they work with brands or not. Next, get in touch with a number of them either via direct instant-messaging or if they have a contact email on their bio, drop them an email introducing your business and find out if they will be happy to promote your business in return for a FREE product?

Chances are they will always say YES. After all who doesn't want a freebie right? However, before you send out any products, it is always a good idea to have some sort of binding contract in place detailing what you have both agreed, prices, how promotion will work, frequency of promotions, etc. It also helps to ask the influencer to send you screenshots of their current traffic and post engagements, videos, etc to help you gauge what type of results to expect from them.

Once they receive the product, all they have to do is take some pictures or videos and post on their page, referring all their fans to your business to purchase the products. Do bear in mind that some of the larger and more established influencers may charge you a fixed fee to promote your company to their audience - but this could be a powerful way to gain brand exposure quickly.

You can also do a Youtube search on your relevant niche and you should find a few different Youtube channels that produce content around your business area. Use search terms such as your niche plus the word reviews, hauls, etc. For example plus size clothing haul, plus size clothing reviews, etc. This will bring up Youtube channels of influencers currently reviewing other products around your niche.

Once the influencer(s) starts posting, you should expect to see an influx of traffic and sales to your website. Using influencer is perfect for especially new businesses to build some social proof around their company ultimately building trust and brand awareness.

IMPORTANT TIP: It is best to work with smaller influencers who are relevant to your niche than larger influencers who are paid by different companies to promote different types of products.

You do not want to work with an influencer that promotes watches today, weight loss products tomorrow and hair bundles the day after simply because they are a LARGE influencer. You will also notice that the engagements their campaigns get usually don't scream interest in what they are promoting.

However if you can find a smaller influencer who focuses solely on the type of products you are selling, you will realise that their audience appears more engaged. **More followers do not equal more Sales**. You want to focus on people that will actually purchase your products, not just random visitors to your website.

If you are interested in learning more in-depth about Influencer Marketing, then checkout the **Run Boutique Business Kit** which contains an in depth marketing course on how everything works.

Email Marketing

Email marketing is a **solid form** of marketing and one that will bring you recurring customers over and over and over again. You obtain their emails and send deals, offers, discounts, promotions to keep them up to date with everything going on.

But how do you get these customers in the first place? One easy way of getting them is asking them to subscribe on your website for updates, discounts and new product releases. This process of getting customers to your list is called **List Building.**

List building is vital for every online business. It is the most effective way of building loyalty and trust with your visitors in the long term. Truth is, most people will come to your website and when they leave, you will never hear back from them ever again or even know they ever visited your site in the first place. However, with list building you can capture their email addresses and get to keep these customers for **GOOD.**

The list building process is used by a lot of multi-million dollar companies to get customers and definitely a marketing strategy we highly recommend. Now when you look back at how much social media has evolved over the years, you will realise that the trends come and go. We had Myspace back in the day, then Hi5, Bebo etc. Nowadays we have moved on to Facebook, Twitter, Instagram, and now Tik Tok seems to be taking over the social marketing space. The lesson to learn here is the fact that social media platforms come and go.

So lets say for example Instagram decides to shut down today, your thousands or millions of followers will vanish just like that. However if you had these people's email addresses then it will be easy for you to keep in contact with them regardless. Hence why Email marketing is still one of the best ways to market any business.

In order to get people's email, you need to capture their attention. A great way to capture people's attention fast is to offer something for FREE or a discount on your services.

Truth is people love freebies and once they see the word FREE, they won't hesitate to grab or come running for those products or services. For your online store, you could offer your customers a discount code in exchange for their email addresses. That way they can sign up to receive a discount off their first order. That's exactly the same way list building works.

Secondly you will also need an autoresponder that can help you automatically deliver your incentive via email marketing to your subscribers once they subscribe. Without an autoresponder, it will be impossible to collect those emails in the first place and send people their discount codes. A great autoresponder software I will highly recommend is **Aweber**. **Aweber** allows you to create pop ups and opt in forms, and automates the email marketing process for you.

Once you have an autoresponder, it's time to create your pop up or sign up form on your website. This is simply a little box asking users for their name and email address in exchange for your free incentive above. Most ecommerce platforms allow you to create pop ups easily.

Once they visit your website, sign up and confirm their subscription, they will then become stored in your list and you can send them regular emails, new product releases, courses, updates and other useful information. This is also used to build strong relationships with your subscribers. Remember you are NOT selling them anything yet but giving them something for free in exchange of their name and email address.

Once you have their email address, it's all about nurturing your subscribers and keeping in touch with them as much as you can - *in a non spammy way of course*. It is advisable to communicate with your email subscribers at least twice a week. If you go too long without speaking to them, they will soon forget about you.

One problem most businesses face is not knowing exactly what emails to send out to their subscribers or sending out emails and not seeing much of a result. Not to worry because we've put together a list of <u>**365+ Catchy Email subject lines**</u> you can send out to your subscribers to keep them engaged and encouraged to open your emails every single time and ultimately drive more sales.

You can gain access to these email scripts plus a more in-depth Email Marketing course at the **Run Boutique Business Kit**.

Poshmark & Depop

People go on platforms such as Poshmark and Depop every single day looking for different types of products to purchase such as; used products, new products, or even clearance stock.

The good thing about working with these platforms is the fact that they are already established and have people who know and trust them well enough to purchase from their platforms. Ofcourse this therefore means FREE promotion for you as a new business just starting out, because you can use these platforms to drive traffic back to your website.

However, because a lot of people come to these platforms looking for a bargain, my advice will be to sell your lower priced products or clearance stock just to build your portfolio and get attention quicker from customers. When a customer buys your low cost products, you then ship the products out to them **TOGETHER WITH YOUR BUSINESS CARD AND FLYERS DIRECTING THEM BACK TO SHOP FROM YOUR WEBSITE IN THE FUTURE**. So you are essentially using those low cost products to create a buzz and get attention quicker. As you store grows and those reviews start piling up on these platforms, you will soon start noticing an influx of traffic back to your website.

You can even leave them a thank you note with a discount code to shop for more great deals on your website. Below is a good example;

*"Hey thanks so much for purchasing from me. If you are interested in more fabulous items like this, then feel free to check out my website at **wyz.cm** where you can get 15% off your next order"*

This means next time, the customer wants some products from you, they will go directly to your website to benefit from that fabulous discount. You now also have the opportunity to grab their email address and market to them over and over again to increase sales in the future.

Fashion Shows & Networking

Attending fashion shows and exhibitions are another great way to expose your business in a place with like-minded people. Truth is people going for these shows have a passion for fashion meaning you can easily connect with them and gain some potential customers for your business.

Business networking is an activity of socioeconomic character, which brings together like minded people or businessmen, to create new business opportunities and also act upon different business ideas.

Networking is a very powerful yet underused method of marketing for most businesses. The truth is if you can meet people face to face and tell them about your exciting business and what you offer, ultimately selling yourself. So research business networking events around your local area, try to attend them, connect with people and don't forget to take along your business cards and or flyers.

Where to Get

Where to get is an amazing platform for every online clothing boutique out there. Basically as the name implies, people go there posting pictures asking **"where to get"** different types of products whilst others post links to websites they can get those products from.

For example I see a gorgeous dress on a celebrity and want to purchase it but don't know "where to get" it. I will simply upload a picture on that website. People then start to respond to it by directing me to different websites where I can get it. As a boutique store owner, you are most likely going to find a lot of direct customers looking for products which you currently sell. So you simply respond to them with a link to your website, they purchase from you, you make money.

Another good thing about this platform is, you can list your own products on your page and refer people to your website who love it. So remember to list your own products with links to your website on your page.

- So go register for a free account at **www.wheretoget.it**

- Once registered click on "Answer" at the top Menu

- You will then be presented with different images posted by people looking for where to get those outfits. If you come across any pictures or products that are similar to what you sell, then simply "Post a Tip" and link them back to your website. Remember if you don't sell the exact product they are looking for, but have something similar, you can always still refer them to this alternative. The more people you help, the more they start to visit your profile and browse through more of your own products and eventually end up on your website.

- You can also open your own shop and list your own products for sale within the platform which is great for driving traffic back to your store.

Pop Up Shops

Pop Up shops are another powerful way to promote and market your new online store.

Pop-up retail is the temporary use of physical space to create a long term, lasting impression with potential customers. A pop-up shop allows you to communicate your brand's promise to your customers through the use of a unique and engaging physical environment while creating an immersive shopping experience (Shopify, 2018).

Truth is there are a lot of people that still want to see, feel, and touch products prior to purchasing them. And having a pop up shop offers just that. To set up a pop up shop you need to start by researching pop ups in your local areas, then get in touch with the venues to secure a space. Alternatively if there are no pop ups in your area, why not set up your own pop up? Simply rent some space and invite other businesses to promote themselves - at a small fee of course. Then promote your event as much as you can and get the ball rolling.

Instagram

Instagram is an online service in video-sharing, photo-sharing and social networking that enables you to take pictures and videos and apply filters to them. You can edit the photos and essentially communicate with your customers via images and video making it a very powerful marketing platform for your business.

Instagram has more than 750 million members that are active on the site, which is more than Twitter. This means more and more brands are discovering how to use Instagram to gain more followers and share their brand message.

If you're not convinced that Instagram would benefit your company, consider this, users of Instagram are buyers. There have been numerous studies done that show them in the last five years alone, Instagram's network has grown in purchasing power by customers, and it will only increase more.

As opposed to the other social media sites that you can utilize for your business, Instagram is wholly comprised of the visual appeal element. Exploring the use of Instagram to grow your brand will force you to think about the visual component to your brand.

1. To get started with instagram, simply register for a free account at www.instagram.com and remember to use our business name as your display name.

2. Once registered you will need to start posting some amazing pictures to attract some likes, views and followers to your page. This can be a picture of the products or services you sell, your blog content etc.

3. Next use hashtags (#) under each post to attract as much engagement as possible. Say for example your business is on plus size clothing, then you could post your content then use popular hashtags around that niche. e.g. #plussizedress #plussizejeans #fplussizefashion, etc.

To find out what hashtags are trending in your niche, simply do a search on instagram with your hashtag and relevant keyword (#plussize) and instagram will begin to recommend the most popular hashtags around your niche as shown below;

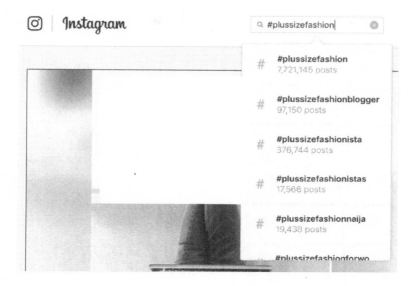

Now take a note of those popular hashtags and list them under your own pictures. This means anyone going on instagram looking for anything fashion related will most likely stumble on your account and eventually follow you. The more followers you get, the more your brand is known and the more exposure it gets.

A second way to gain engagement fast is to look at your competitors accounts, then find out who their followers are, next follow their followers and in return they will begin to follow you too.

Remember to also leave comments under their pictures to build and drive engagement and of course get them curious to check you out.

Another way to gain engagement fast on instagram is to follow accounts of your target audience. Again if you know exactly who your customer is, then it will be easier for you to find them on instagram.

For example, if your target audience is the woman who works for herself, then you can search for keywords like #girlboss #femaleentrepreneur #womeninbusiness #bossbabe etc. Think about their personality and what type of hashtags they are likely to use in their instagram posts. Connect with them and build engagement and your following and client base will grow before you know it.

This might take a while initially, but can get you so many free and unique visitors to your page and consequently to your business. And remember, you only have to do this once until your account starts to grow and build momentum.

If you can invest time initially or better still hire a social media manager or virtual assistant to help you if struggling - so many can be found at www.fiverr.com and only charge per project. So you aren't actually hiring anyone full time which is a plus to you as a new business.

Below are a few useful Instagram Marketing Tips:

- Don't like so many pictures within an hour (e.g. liking over 100 pictures per hour could get instagram to think you are spamming and in the unfortunate circumstances might block your account).

- Don't post pictures promoting products or services all the time. Mix and match both formal and informal pictures. Memes, quotes, behind the scenes photoshoot videos etc.

- Be consistent! Post at-least once a day and spend a few minutes each day liking pictures of people with an interest in your niche. Even comment in their pictures to draw even more attention back to your own page.

- Remember to post your website url link in the bio so people can easily visit your website and purchase your products. Your Instagram profile is the one place where your connections with other members are interactive, directly under your name and description at the highest point of your page. Within this area, you can post a link to your business site or a landing page for your products. Keeping a link to either of these two places can help you boost targeted traffic to your site

- To grow and promote your instagram account even faster, you can use an online service like Iconosquare, which provides several tools and resources to help with your social media marketing.

- Make sure you post at the right time. As will all of the social networking platforms, you need to post your content at the right time. According to SimplyMeasured, an analytics company, the best time to post to Instagram is on Wednesdays

between 5 and 6 p.m.

⬜ When scheduling your posts, you want to be sure you are aware of when your target audience will most likely be online and on Instagram. It helps you in judging the best time to post and act accordingly. One of the best websites for choosing the peak times for increasing engagement is **IconoSquare**, which gives an optimization report based on one's participation and posting history in the past. With <u>IconoSquare</u>, you get a detailed report in which black circles represent the times that you're posting, and light-gray circles that represent the level of engagement the posts received in the past. The best times or the peak times to post are shown by the most prominent light-gray circles, which are calculated based on your followers' engagement on the site.

If you are interested in learning more in-depth about Instagram Marketing plus access to our social media content planner kit, then checkout the <u>**Run Boutique Business Kit**</u> which contains all these tools and resources.

Search Engine Optimization

Search Engine Optimization is still one of the most powerful ways to drive FREE and targeted traffic to your website from people with a genuine interest in your products. The secret with getting more traffic to your store using search engine optimization is to use the correct terms or keywords that people are searching for the products you're selling.

For example, assuming you are selling plus size clothing, then you want to make sure you use the <u>Google Keyword Tool</u> to find out what people are looking for around the plus size clothing. Another great plugin you can upload to your Google Chrome browser is the <u>Keywords Everywhere</u> plugin which basically brings up keyword suggestions relevant to your search as shown below.

As you can see on the right hand side of the screen, there are several keyword suggestions of what people are searching for around the cat plus size clothing. These are keywords you can use on your product titles, descriptions, tags and listings to help rank your website at the top of the Google search engine. This means when people go on google searching for plus size clothing, your website will begin to rank at the top of the search engine thereby bringing you FREE and targeted traffic. Now that's the power of SEO (Search Engine Optimization).

If you are interested in learning more in-depth about SEO Marketing, then checkout the **Run Boutique Business Kit** which contains more information.

Pinterest

Pinterest is another powerful way of reaching out to thousands of customers online easily. People go on Pinterest every single day looking for inspiration and ideas on different things, from fashion ideas to weight loss recipes. Content is usually shared in the form of **pins** and **boards.** You can think of your board as an "Album" and your pins as the "Images" within that album.

So how is this beneficial to your business? Now assuming your online boutique was centred on "plus size clothing", then what you could do is register for a free Pinterest account and upload product images from your website. This means if someone went on Pinterest (or even google) searching for ideas around plus size clothing, then your pins or boards are likely show up, thereby linking them back to your website and consequently winning you a new customer. This works just like search engine optimization and can generate ongoing FREE website traffic for your business every single day.

To get started with Pinterest, register for a FREE account at: https://www.pinterest.com. Once registered, you can begin creating boards and pins with your images and relevant content.

You can upload product images directly from your website into your Pinterest boards. Remember to use the right titles and descriptions on your products in order to attract your target audience who are likely to find you easily not only through Pinterest, but also from doing Google searches. The best way to find the right keywords again is following the steps we previously outlined on search engine optimization - remember Pinterest is also a Search Engine. Each time you have some new products on your online store, remember to upload some product pins in your account to link them back to your online store.

Here are some useful tips to take into account when using Pinterest;

Create Boards that Include Keywords in the Title

Pinterest has terrific search capabilities. In order to bring even more people to learn about your business, you'll want to include relevant keywords in the titles of your boards. You want to be sure that you choose a category for each of your boards, as well as utilizing the option for Pinterest to suggest your boards. This way you'll be found much quicker and easier by your target audience. And remember not to set your boards as private.

Descriptions

When writing the description for your boards, it is imperative that you utilize relevant SEO friendly keywords. You want to keep in mind that users can tweet and share your pins via Facebook, so by using keywords, your pins can be more easily searched on these other social media sites.

Plus, what you write in the description is what becomes the tweet, so you'll need to keep the description brief, appealing, and relevant.

Use Vertical Images

In order to take up the most considerable amount of visual space, the images you add to Pinterest should be long and narrow. Look through the site and note what your competitors pins have in common and then apply the same techniques to your images.

You will be able to recognize the kinds of images that are most repinned and shared. Most users don't include a big image but have one that pins with every post. Remember pictures are worth a thousand words.

Utilize Rich Pins

In 2015, Pinterest introduced buyable pins that contain more information than a regular link. Rich pins allow users to buy things directly from other users that utilize this feature. With rich pins, users are able to see prices and select a particular product, choose the color or size, and whatever that specific product includes, and then press a button to buy the product.

There are five kinds of Rich Pins that you can take advantage of at the moment. They include movies, recipes, articles, **products,** and places. Your business can advertise almost everything, and almost everything can be bought. Take the time to find your chosen Rich Pins and apply to get them. If you're not skilled, you can ask your site developer or site owner to help you get what you're looking for.

If you are interested in learning more in-depth about Pinterest Marketing, then checkout the **Run Boutique Business Kit** which contains more information.

Amazon FBA

Now if you live on this planet, then I'm sure you've heard about Amazon before. Amazon is the largest ecommerce platform in the world right now with billions of sellers selling products there and billions of buyers visiting the platform every single month. Amazon now has an FBA program which means - Fulfilled By Amazon. So as the name implies, Amazon is responsible for fulfilling your orders. Now using the Amazon FBA program is a great way to sell your inventory extremely fast without going through the stress of packaging and shipping out orders.

So what you could do is simply ship your inventory out to an Amazon warehouse closest to you (Amazon will usually provide you the address when you sign up), next list your products for sale in your Amazon shop. When a customer buys your product, Amazon automatically deals with the fulfilment and shipping of the product directly to your customer. You can even get your suppliers to send your inventory directly to the Amazon warehouse in the future, meaning there's no need for you to lift a single finger.

And because Amazon is already a well known and trusted platform, your products will start attracting FREE traffic and sales without you having to do much. Using Amazon FBA is certainly a powerful way to market your store and increase sales fast.

One thing to note however is that you will need to pay a monthly membership fee of $39.99 as a professional seller which honestly cannot be compared to how much you will probably spend monthly trying to market your boutique or store using other strategies. When sending out your inventory to Amazon, the trick is to include as much of your branding and business details as possible in your packages. This could be through flyers, thank you cards, business cards, label tags and anything that has your website information on it.

That way when customers receive their packages from Amazon, they will come back to shop directly from you in the future - especially if you are offering them more variety, better deals in your store than what they are getting on Amazon. Again you could even test this process out by sending out your old stock or inventory you are struggling to sell - which of course can be priced lower as a way to get customers fast and build brand reputation. Then use that to drive people to your website to purchase your high end products.

This is a hot strategy that not so many store owners use and one that can drive thousands of sales and customers back to your store. You can get started with the Amazon FBA program by **CLICKING HERE**.

Affiliate Marketing

Another powerful way to get free traffic to your online store is using affiliate marketing. Affiliates are companies, individuals and organizations that you have established business relationships with in order to increase your exposure and sales revenue.

Affiliates send traffic to your site via a link representing your business on their site. If the prospective customer should buy from you the affiliate gets a commission from the transaction. In order to use affiliates you are required to register with an affiliate program and begin recruiting affiliates to work for you.

Offering a handsome commission can attract affiliates to sign up to your program. Having a professional website that will be easy for them to integrate with their own site can also peak the interests of potential affiliates. As a store owner, this means FREE traffic to your online store every single day.

You can create your own affiliate program on most ecommerce platforms such as Shopify, Woocommerce etc, or alternatively checkout external third party affiliate websites such as **Awin**, **Shareasale** , **CJ.COM** etc.

If you need more in-depth step by step information around Affiliate Marketing, then checkout the **Run Boutique Business Kit** where we explain in more detail through our training videos how everything works.

Facebook

Facebook is a social network and micro-blogging platform with a leading social community online. As a matter of fact, there are currently over 1.6 billion active users on facebook. Having a Facebook page for your business is a great way to build relationships with existing clients, communicate with them, win new clients, interact and engage with all your customers. Once people are able to relate with you, winning those customers to your business and making sales will be easier than you think.

Facebook is free to join and also very search engine friendly. The truth is google will sometimes target your Facebook page even better than your website. This means opening your Facebook page with your business name will ensure your business is ranked at the top of google. "Why not try this and see how fast google ranks your business".

Compared to other traditional advertising strategies out there, Facebook is not only free to use but is a cheaper way to advertise your business to an even wider audience. Not only do you attract a wider audience, you can easily track performance to see how well your ads are performing and where traffic is coming from.

One of the greatest things about advertising with

Facebook, is the flexibility of your advertisements. You can customize your advertisements so they appear only to specific groups or segments of people based on the information contained within their profile or based on gender, location or personal preference.

Unlike profiles, business pages are public, which means anyone can follow a link to see everything that has been posted on the page. With a business page, you can also set up paid advertising for both Facebook and Instagram.

Getting Started on Facebook

In-order to start advertising your business on Facebook, you must first of all create a personal facebook account. Once you have a personal account set up then open a business page on facebook.

1. If you don't already have a facebook account, register a FREE account at www.facebook.com. You will then be prompted to complete all the relevant information to enable you to create an account. Please **DO NOT** use your personal account for business.

2. Once you create a personal account, the next step

is to create a business page. Click on the drop down Arrow at the top Right hand of the page and click on **"Create Page"**.

3. You can then select the relevant page from business, brand, company etc., depending on your business type.

4. Fill out all the relevant information about your business, brand or company. On the **"enter an address for your page field"** type in your exact company name.

This will ensure your business page is properly ranked by Google.

5. Next upload a profile picture for your business. If you are a company or brand, then your logo is usually the best option. If your face is your brand, then a good professional picture of you should do the trick.

6. Next add a great cover picture on your page. Make sure your cover picture is professionally designed and can stand out in order to attract customers and people to your page.

7. Guess what? **You have just created your facebook**

page for your business in just minutes.

You can advertise through Facebook using three different methods;

Freely – promote your facebook page to your existing customers and grow your page organically.

Facebook Ads – pay Facebook to attract millions of customers for you on your behalf.

Facebook Groups – Join groups similar to your niche, participate with others and use that to promote your services.

Once you have your page created, the next step is to invite your customers, clients and friends to like your page. You can easily get fans and followers to your facebook page by connecting your Facebook page to your website.

This means your website visitors get to find your new facebook page and like it. If you already have friends on facebook, you could also invite your friends to like your page and get them to spread the word. Now it's time to start posting on facebook and attracting some new fans to your page. Be aware that opening a facebook page for the sake of just opening a page won't drive any customers to your business. In fact you are better off not opening a page in the first place if you intend to just abandon it and expect sales. While you may have a Facebook page for your business, the question becomes whether or not you are using it to its fullest. Facebook is a great tool that can be used to effectively grow your business with a lot less effort than you've been putting in up until now. In addition to posting updates about your business, there are numerous ways that you can utilize your Facebook page to create awareness among your audience to spread brand awareness and gain more followers.

Here are some of the most effective ways that you can use your Facebook business page to grow your brand awareness and gain more traffic to your company website;

Ask for Testimonials and Reviews

To improve your brand name and spread awareness about your company, it can help a great deal if you post testimonials and reviews on your business page. Apart from having a Facebook page filled with the reviews of your customers, you can also select some of the best reviews and post them on your website so visitors can see what others are saying.

Engage with Your Audience

An essential element of using your Facebook page for your business is connecting with your audience. Your audience on Facebook will consist of fans of your business, fans of your content, current and former customers, as well as potential customers. When you post content on your page, you need to keep this in mind, because your first priority is to connect with your audience.

If you follow the traditional method of audience engagement, you should be following the 80/20 rule. This means that 80 percent of the content that you post should be value-added content with the remaining 20 percent promoting your business. You can fill the 20 percent with material that is used for marketing, sales, or self-promotion purposes.

It is imperative to engage with your audience if you want to promote your business page. The best way to catch their attention is by posting unique and informative content that is related to your business or industry. To win a loyal and engaged audience for your business, you have to create content that is relevant to your niche.

It is also critical to interact with your audience. This can be done by providing them with the kind of content they desire, as well as replying to the comments they post to your page. To ensure that you produce content that will engage your audience, monitor the comments that are posted so you can find out what your audience likes or doesn't like about what you've posted.

Ask for Customer Feedback

It is always best for your business to get a clear understanding of your customer's expectations and then to strive to fulfill their demands. The best way to get an accurate understanding of how current and potential customers feel about your brand or product is to survey them. Not only does polling your audience give you a path to connect with your customers, but it also helps you understand what your customer's expectations in a much better way.

If you find creating a survey is too time-consuming, Facebook has made it easy for users to create simple polls with their Facebook polling app. The app allows you to create a simple to use survey which can be easily understood by your audience. The best thing about the app is that it will provide you with readymade answers and can collect personal information in a way that will satisfy any privacy concerns that might arise.

Offer Helpful Resources

The best way to grow your audience and get more targeted traffic to your business site is to offer resources to your audience. Providing your audience with helpful and value-added resources will also help to set you up as an authority and thought leader in your industry.

Some of the best posts that you should be sharing on your business page is breaking news, blog posts, new tools, features, and products, book recommendation, and other useful websites.

Use Images in Your Posts

Photos are an extraordinary addition to your Facebook posts. So you want to post the highest number of pictures as you can. Not only can images convey a wide range of information, but it can also focus on a single thought or emotion. Recent studies have also determined that images get shared more often than posts that contain only text. The best part about adding images to your Facebook business page is that they don't need to be created by an expert. You can post images of your products, behind the scenes of your photoshoots and other images that will connect with your customers at a more personal level with your business.

If you need a more in-depth step by step training course on Facebook Marketing, then checkout the **Run Boutique Business Kit** where we explain in more detail through our training videos how everything works.

Referrals

Referrals are a method of spreading the word by telling a friend to tell a friend. Let people know about your new business and let your friends tell others about your business. Referral marketing is a structured and systematic process to maximize word of mouth potential. Referral marketing does this by encouraging, informing, promoting and rewarding customers and contacts to think and talk as much as possible about their supplier, their company, product and service and the value and benefit the supplier brings to them and people they know.

Word of mouth is potentially the best form of marketing for a business and best of all, is probably the most cost effective! Also known as viral marketing, word of mouth lets your customers do the promotion for you which is the best recommendation that anyone can get. The BEST way to get people talking about your services is to GIVE them value first. The best sources for your referrals are your existing customers – these are the people who are loyal to you and have trusted you well enough to purchase from you.

A few ways to get them to refer to your brand is to offer them customers' discounts and rewards each time they refer a new friend to your boutique. Alternatively get them to leave reviews in exchange for an incentive.

That is how you get word of mouth going and get the attention of potential clients. Thereafter, it's just a matter of building a friendly relationship (not hard selling) with the people you meet and/or already know.

You'll be amazed at how easy it is and what great connections you'll make, along with the opportunities that will open up and bring you more clients!

FINALLY...

Remember these marketing strategies are all powerful in their own right. You do not necessarily need to implement all these strategies but rather focus on the strategies most relevant to your business. If you require more in-depth training courses on these different marketing strategies work, then checkout the "**_Run Boutique Business Kit_**" at;

www.runboutiqueacademy.com

Part 8

POSITIONING YOURSELF FOR SUCCESS

Congratulations on making it this far! Hopefully you should have your new online clothing boutique up and running by now - or at least have some ideas to get you in the process. You will be pleased to know that, you've officially gone through the most important steps towards starting your online clothing boutique.

Like most business books out there, I could easily end this book right here and leave the rest to you which is fine. However from experience, I can assure you that there is more to business than just coming up with an idea, starting that business and attracting customers.

This is something so many business owners are unaware of, and reason most people find themselves stuck after starting a business whilst others give up before they've even started the business.

Now that you finally have a business up and running and some marketing strategies in place, this is sufficient to keep you going. However in-order to run a business successfully, you need to look into effective ways of positioning yourself for long term business success which is exactly what this chapter aims to explore.

Staying Creative and Innovative

Coming up with a business idea is a great first step towards tapping into your creative juices. However creativity shouldn't just end at coming up with an idea but you should consistently seek for more innovative ways to improve and grow your business. When innovation and creativity stops in a business, it reflects negatively on business success.

You do not require a special skill or talent in-order to be creative. You can be creative even if you don't think you are - everyone can be creative but you have to be willing to start somewhere and the creative process will become more natural over time. Below are a few tips and habits to help you stay creative in your business.

Make New Connections: Being innovative doesn't require a university degree; it simply requires making a connection between existing ideas. For example a self-service checkout installed in a supermarket doesn't change the idea of the supermarket but rather a process in that existing supermarket.

So look at your existing business or others around you and see how processes could be improved and things done differently.

Think Outside The Box: Many of the products we take for granted today are the result of people thinking outside their limits. E.g. The smartphone is now part of our day to day lives, however it took an innovative and creative person to come up with that idea of changing the way we use our phones.

Ask Questions: Creative thinking goes beyond just solving specific problems or inventing new things. A truly creative mind is always coming up with the questions too, not just the solutions. What questions are you asking to prompt your ideas? The larger the question, the larger the impact those ideas may have on the world. You can start by addressing smaller problems but don't limit yourself to those.

Think Like A Child: As adults we tend to think in a conditioned way aimed at showing how clever we are. Yet, as children, we were simply spontaneous and far more creative in our thinking. To recapture your childhood curiosity, allow yourself to just wonder at things, to be completely present in the here and now, and to detach yourself from what you thought was real.

Note down your Ideas: Personally my creative juices tend to flow in during the late hours of the night just before I snooze to sleep. What I then do is, immediately type out those ideas on my phone notepad because trust me it is very easy to forget those ideas. Choose what works best for you and make sure you have a way to record your ideas at all times. You never know when an important idea will surface. Capture all of your ideas - even those that seem impossible to implement at that time, because what seems impossible now may not be impossible in the future.

Set Goals

Goal setting is extremely useful in positioning yourself for business success. Every business has a mission and a vision which you need to be working towards at all times. The moment you lose focus of these goals is the moment your business starts to suffer. Think of a football game for example;

"People play football with the goal of scoring. If there wasn't a goal to score, then football might just be a pointless sport".

So like football setting goals be it for your life, your career or your business is key to achieving long term success. Goals are a great tool for direction and also provide the motivation to get us through difficult times and choices. For example going to college while working full-time may be stressful and difficult in the short-term, but in the long run being able to pursue the professional goals we desire will make it worthwhile. Goals also serve as the destination for what we really want out of life.

For some people, goals are measured in money or material goods, while for others goals are measured in time or freedom. You will never achieve your goals unless you: *know exactly what you want, are passionate about your goal, and have a solid, realistic plan of action*. However do not fall into the temptation of only focusing on your long term goals and losing sight of your short term goals. The reason some people find it too hard to achieve their goals is because they tend to set their long term goals, prior to setting their short term goals or simply not planning out their goals carefully. Short-term goals seem to be our starting point for our long term ones and can also motivate one to plan for longer goals, so make sure you start with your short term goals first.

Another important step in goal setting is to identify exactly what your goal is. What will achieving that goal really look like? Be as specific as possible about exactly what your desired end result is. If your goal is to create a more successful business, what will that look like? Are you thinking in terms of simply hiring someone else to give you more free time? Are you looking for more sales and profit?

Regardless of what you want, the best way to get it is to first clarify exactly what you want in as much detail as possible. This may seem like hard work - but without a clear mental picture, you'll never have the focus required to achieve your goal. Next remember to write down your goals in as much detail as possible. Then ensure that you review and revisit them on a daily to weekly basis because this will encourage and motivate you to achieve them, plus this will also keep that vision of your goal alive.

Sharing your goals with someone you trust or even a mentor is another great way to set goals. By sharing your goals with other people you can get a second opinion which could help you in that journey of success. The problem that usually occurs though is that, some people are just too shy to tell others about their goals for several reasons which is quite understandable. However, if there's someone you feel you can trust to share your goals with, then do not hold back on another view point.

Finally, remember not to lose track. It is very possible that at some point in your business journey, you might realise that you are not achieving your goals as well or as quickly as you had initially anticipated. However do not let this discourage you but rather pick up where you left off or find other effective ways to achieve that goal.

Time Management is Key

If you are like me, then you've probably had those moments where it felt like there just wasn't enough hours in the day. So much to do but yet so little time to achieve it all. Somehow there never seems to be enough time to get everything done especially given the fact that we just have about 16 hours a day not counting 8 hours of sleep time, it's important how we use the time we have - especially as entrepreneurs.

From dealing with customer service to managing finances, marketing and advertising etc - running a business comes with so many hurdles that can make the whole process all too overwhelming for most entrepreneurs. One has to be committed to fulfill all the responsibilities with 100% perfection and in doing so, people find themselves perplexed as to how to approach and manage all the things and still enjoy ample leisure hours.

Sometimes it may even feel like you are working for hours without any results - especially during the initial stages of your business.

As such time management is key and you need to find a way to discipline yourself.

Setting specific working hours is one essential way to overcome this problem. This would provide an outline, on the basis of which further planning would be undertaken especially given that it is so easy to waste working time on non-productive tasks unconsciously. Personally I have a weekly timetable set up with hours of work and what I need to do each day. For example, Monday mornings are for creating content, whilst afternoons are for business improvement processes. However I still occasionally get distracted by client calls, etc which are unavoidable, but I always find ways to get back on track. Hence, flexibility has to be exercised when managing time, as the actual time taken could be different from planned.

Secondly, set yourself some break hours. It is very easy especially for us entrepreneurs to spend the whole day and night on our computer screens. There's a reason why even 9-5 jobs come with breaks - because these are great to get yourself out of your desk and recharge your batteries. Similarly, you should set yourself some hours in the day where you can unwind, relax, go for a walk and just give yourself a break. Another important aspect of time management is setting priorities to ensure tasks are performed in order of priority. Prior to me outsourcing my customer service to virtual assistants, I used to spend almost half my day responding to customer queries back and forth. I would feel like I had to respond to those emails as soon as possible otherwise I would lose a potential client. Now there's a reason why even larger companies have service level agreement (SLA) times. So I decided to set a response time of 48 hours, then created an autoresponder which immediately told my customers their queries will be picked up within that time. This meant that I could give myself a break, then pick up the queries at the times I had set for myself - trust me those customers can wait especially if their queries are non-urgent! So set specific times during your work hours to open email. This should usually be the first thing and the last thing you do each work day. If you open your email periodically and respond to it, your work hours can be eaten up in a hurry!

Staying Motivated

As a business owner, staying motivated can sometimes be one of the hardest things to emulate - especially during those times when it seems business just isn't going as planned. After all, how do you really stay motivated when you are so close to losing the will to carry on with that business? Lack of motivation happens to us all, but if you do not encourage yourself to accept opportunities and be challenged, no one else will. It is most important to keep your eye on the goal, find ways to keep going, and in no time, you shall reap its benefits. The truth is, the biggest things usually happen when we are at the verge of giving up or quitting. After all pain is one of those things that forces people to change.

For example; getting a negative customer review might just be the push you need to improve your business. Not making any sales might actually motivate you to invest more on your marketing and advertising strategies, etc. It may seem like a bitter experience at first but it's just the right amount of motivation we need in order to improve our business and even ourselves.

I remember it took me a year of going back and forth to finally start this book, and another 8 months or so to eventually complete it. Although the idea was always in mind, I would often find myself struggling to complete a single page, then will find myself leaving it for some few weeks or so before I could even force myself to continue writing the book. At the time it was just a book idea but there was really nothing motivating or pushing me to complete the book, until I started receiving countless queries from clients needing help with starting their online boutique. Finally committed to a group of people who were constantly asking me when the book will be out, I had no choice but to commit to the writing of the book - there was no turning back. Every time I felt demotivated to write, I would think about all those people waiting for the book to be launched and this will instantly motivate me to keep going. This was the push I needed to keep the book going.

So like me, you need to constantly remind yourself about why you are doing it? Who are you doing it for? Why are you even running that business or project? What pushed you to start that business in the first place?

Is it to create your own business empire, become your own boss, quit that stressful job or just spend more time with your family and loved ones? What were those missions and visions you initially set out to achieve? Do they still stand or have these changed and why? Find something to keep you motivated and always stay focused on that goal.

To motivate yourself, sometimes you need to be willing to step out of your comfort zone because success like they say only begins outside your comfort zone. Be willing to push yourself beyond the norm - no matter how strange or abnormal it may seem.

Don't lose focus on your goal and use that to stay motivated. Keep believing in yourself and your ability to achieve success, avoid negativity, toxic people and anything that will hinder your success or hold you back, avoid distractions, hang on to your dreams - they may dangle in there for a moment but these little stars will be your driving force.

Give yourself a break, exercise regularly, have enough rest, take sufficient sleep and recharge yourself after a hard day's work. Keep trying no matter how hard life may seem and remember winners never quit.

Self Improvement

One of my favourite quotes by Warren Buffett is the one which goes;

"The more you learn the more you earn".

Business is something that is constantly changing especially given the digital era we now live in with constant changes, technological upgrades, new systems, new social media platforms, etc which can all impact business operations.

The truth is, marketing strategies that worked 4-5 years ago may not be as effective today as they were back in the day.

For example, traditional marketing strategies such as cold calling, direct mail marketing are close to non-effective these days due to emerging digital trends such as social media marketing, which have now transformed the way businesses are run and operated. Online shopping is another trend transforming the way traditional businesses operate. It is very rare to find a business these days that lacks an online presence - and if it does, there's a high chance this could be hindering their sales and growth drastically.

Personally I am constantly investing time and money in learning new skills and working on business improvement through self-development. When I went back to university to complete my Masters in Business Management with Entrepreneurship in 2017, people kept asking me;

"What's the point of doing a masters when you already have thriving businesses up and running?"

My answer always remained, I need to learn more new and transferable skills that could help improve my businesses.

Bear in mind my background was Accounting and Finance, and although I had some experience starting several businesses, I was still lacking on other business areas, hence decided to take on the course. Not only has this course helped exposed me to so many new business strategies, it has also helped with self-development and business improvement.

The truth is starting a business is just the tip of the iceberg, however to run a successful business you need to find ways to constantly learn and improve your skills. Now I'm not saying you should go back to university and complete a full time master's programme - there is so much freely accessible information around in the form of google, books, online courses, Youtube and so much more.

Just get on google right now and search for any business related question, and you will be surprised at the amount of FREE information readily available at your fingertips. My point is if your business is still living in the Stone Age or using outdated practices, you will find yourself left behind and your customers will eventually go to your competitors who are more in tune with external changes. For example with my online courses, I cannot count how many times

I've changed and updated its content due to frequent changes around the industry.

So invest a few hours a week learning a new skill that could be beneficial in improving your business. Listen to inspirational speakers, coaches, mentors and other people you look up to in the industry. What are they doing well and how could you achieve the same for your business?

If it means investing in books, courses, training programs to learn and improve your skills, then go for it. Do not underestimate the power of learning for self-improvement and development.

Change is the only constant in life, but one's ability to adapt to it is what will determine your success in life - **Benjamin Franklin**

Productivity is Vital

You might have heard of the saying *"Focus on being productive rather than busy"*. You could be the most hardworking person out there but at the end of the day, productivity depends on how many completed tasks are of good quality. If you do your job right, your overall productivity levels tend to increase.

One great way of staying productive is to be organized. This could be achieved through filing and organizing your paperwork, decluttering, keeping a calendar, etc. In doing so you would realise that you are a lot more productive.

If your environment or workplace is cluttered, then this could equally clutter your mind, your thoughts and your decisions. Hence staying organised is an essential part of staying productive.

Procrastination is a killer as they say and can equally hinder your productivity. If you keep postponing tasks and not taking any action, there is no way you can achieve productivity. Postponing tasks for a day is likely to turn to a week, a month, and eventually never completed. Remember the one thing you can never get back in life is your time. So why waste time procrastinating when you can just get started now!

Too busy? Well who isn't? There are a lot of people out there busier than you who are still able to achieve things and get things done. The time you spend complaining about being too busy is the same time you could spend doing something productive in your life or business. How many hours a week do you spend browsing on social media, watching Netflix, TV, going out there socializing with friends or just complaining about being busy? Surely there are a bunch of unproductive things in your life right now that you could substitute with more productive tasks. Now think about that!

Negative influences in your life are another killer of productivity. To attain continuous productivity, it is very important for you to veer away from people who have negative vibes, constantly bring you down, do not support you, or just don't understand your journey.

It is essential to find a good company of people who are all enthusiastic, encouraging, and have a positive outlook in life to help you stay productive. I've realised that, the older I get, the smaller my circle of friends is becoming.

This is because I am now in a different phase and journey in my life and this change is equally reflected within my social circle. A lot of people I knew in school, college, etc are no longer in contact with me and vice versa, simply because we are all at different stages in our lives and pursuing different interests - which is all part of change and growing up. So if you find yourself still doing the same thing you were doing 5-10 years ago then maybe it's time revisit your goals and ambitions *(or set some if you don't have one)* see what's going right, wrong or what is simply not working? And ask yourself if you are truly achieving productivity or not? And then start finding ways to achieve it.

And finally don't forget to look after your health! One thing I will tell you from experience is that an unhealthy mind and lifestyle equals an unproductive one. I remember there were days where I would overwork myself and get little to no sleep whatsoever and this eventually reflected on my health and most of all productivity. Don't try to fight sleep when it comes knocking - it's your body's way of telling you it's had enough and can't process any more. I used to try and fight sleep by drinking lots of caffeine in the hopes that I would stay awake and achieve more. But the truth is, it was in fact taking me 3-4 hours to complete tasks I'm used to completing in the space of less than an hour - when well rested. So stop lying to yourself that you can be productive despite feeling tired because your brain will never process things as normal or as quickly as it would if you had a good night's rest. It's not worth it! And remember success won't matter if you don't have good health to enjoy it.

Patience is Key

One thing so many of us human beings lack is patience and wanting things to happen when, where and how we expect them to happen. When it comes to business, patience is one of the biggest problems and challenges a lot of entrepreneurs are equally faced with. They start a business today then expect to make their first million by the end of the first month.

And when they don't achieve the results they initially anticipated, they quickly give up in search for the next magical quick fix. Success isn't an overnight process and even the few people who eventually make it to the top, had to go through a process to get to that point and level of success.

For example I've been online since 2012 part time back and forth, and it wasn't until around 2016 that my businesses started generating me a full time income which then allowed me to quit my job and focus on my businesses full time. The reason why it took long for me was because I was basically testing the waters and only doing this part time.

Secondly, I had no one to really guide me in the process and pretty much had to learn from my failures and mistakes as I went along. However this process may be different for you and may not take that long for you to start achieving results especially with a book like this one to guide you, and so many resources now available to speed up this process that weren't available when I initially started.

Furthermore, always remember that your money would not automatically start working for you overnight - it may take a day, a week, a month and even a year depending on how well you treat your business and how you chose to implement the relevant strategies.

If things aren't going as planned, don't give up! Just because it isn't working now doesn't mean it's not going to work tomorrow. Don't quit your day job just yet but rather run your online business part time - evenings and weekends, dedicate a few hours a week building your online business, and as time goes on things will start to fall in place. By keeping your day job, the financial strain isn't too heavy on you either since you can still afford to pay your bills, whilst building additional wealth at the side.

Final Words of Wisdom

Although this book is aimed at ensuring that you take action and implement the relevant strategies necessary to start your online clothing boutique, I understand that life can get in the way of most people. So if you get to a point where you find yourself distracted do not worry, simply pick up from where you left off the day before and continue from there.

Secondly I also understand that everyone is different and some people are at different stages in their startup journey and therefore do not expect you to follow each step as described. So feel free to read and use this book as you please – be it in a day, week, month or year. It's really up to you how you choose to read, use and apply it.

Just remember that the end goal here is to TAKE ACTION.

Starting a business may seem overwhelming at first, but I can assure you that it will all be worth it in the end. The most important thing is taking those first steps towards getting started. Thinking or dreaming about starting a business won't make a difference unless you physically take action. We all have the potential to make our dreams come true and live a more financially fulfilled life.

Remember to stay focused, motivated, productive, patient, creative and keep going. Go start that online clothing boutique right now, don't get left behind whilst others are achieving success. You can either take no action, and stay where you are right now OR turn your life around and start creating that successful business empire. **The ball is now in your court!**

Acknowledgements

Firstly I would like to thank the almighty God for granting me strength and wisdom throughout the process of writing this book. To my amazing parents, family and husband for supporting me morally and emotionally.

To all my clients, students and everyone who has motivated me to write this book – a massive thanks. Finally for all future online boutique owners out there reading this book, I hope you find this book useful in helping you start your own online clothing boutique business from scratch.

Wishing you all the best in your business journey!

Denise.xx

About the Author

Denise Fonweban-Ulasi is an online entrepreneur and business coach. She started her first ever online business in 2012 selling information products online, but has since personally founded several online businesses including her online stores **Yes Weave** – an online hair extension company, and her online clothing brand for professional woman - **Fash Vie**. She is also the founder of the **Run Boutique Academy** - an online platform that offers video courses for people looking into starting their own online clothing boutiques from scratch.

She has over 10 years' of combined experience working within the digital, financial, retail and banking sectors – with 6 years working within the online and digital sectors. Additionally she holds a first class honours degree in Accounting with Entrepreneurship as well as an Msc in Business Management with Entrepreneurship, and a wide range of experience working with entrepreneurs and start-ups as a digital consultant.

With close to 500,000 views on her Youtube channel - the Startup Reine, and so much success in the digital space, her aim is now to build a community, inspire and empower others (especially women like her) into starting their own online businesses, creating success in their life and making their money work for them.

Important Next Steps

Now that you've read this book, you should have pretty much everything you need to start and launch your own successful online clothing boutique. However if you are looking for an all in one boutique business kit that contains more in depth training courses, vendor lists, templates, finance spreadsheets, inventory management spreadsheets, social media content planners and much more, then check out the Run Boutique Business Kit. The Run Boutique Business kitis an all-in-one boutique business kit that contains everything you need to start, launch and run your own successful online boutique right from the comfort of your own home.

This Run Boutique Business KIT includes;

- How to Start an Online Boutique Online Course

- How to Market Your Boutique - Online Course

- A Guide to Dropshipping- Online Course

- 120+ Wholesale and Dropshipping Suppliers

- Online Boutique CEO - eBook (currently an Amazon Bestseller)

- A Guide to Getting 10K paying Customers per month eBook

- A 12 month Social Media Content Planner and Calendar plus Readymade Done for you templates to post consistently on Social Media.

- 365+ Catchy Email Subject Lines to send your email subscribers.

- The Boutique Business Planner Checklist

- Accounts and Bookkeeping Spreadsheet

- Inventory Management Spreadsheet

You also get to join our community of like minded online boutique owners, ask any questions and interact directly with me all the way. You can find out more by visiting:

www.runboutiqueacademy.com

Below are some of the reviews from just a few of our current members on board;

Doyin Omo Jesu
October 15 at 11:39 AM

•••

I was always confused of where and how to start online boutique but since i joined the club it has helped me greatly. I always look forward for the each lesson everyday and enjoyed the simplicity of the lessons which is crucial for starters. I highly recommend Run Boutique club for anyone struggling out there. Thanks Denise, you are a great coach!😄

👍❤ 5   Seen by 5

Gina Marie Schmolze-Whitaker
12 hrs

•••

I want to personally thank Denise for all her expertise she is giving us for FREE!! Helping others to reach their dreams and and helping us all succede🖤🖤You truly are amazing!! Thank you for this site and all the Utube videos u have out there thus far... I've been learning so much from you!! Thank you for YOU🖤🖤🖤

Schamlain Gathright ▶ **Start Online Boutique Members**

4 mins ·

Im learning so much from the Run BOUTIQUE membership.A great investment thus far for me.A great platform to learn alot Thanks Denise.

👍 Like   💬 Comment   ▾

 Write a comment...   ☺ 📷 GIF 🗨

Jennifer Coreah is ☺ feeling happy.

Just now

So glad I stumbled upon the Run Boutique Members Club whilst looking for information on starting my own online boutique. Signed up for the FREE course, then decided to join the VIP membership after it launched and must say it has been the best investment thus far. Not only has this course helped me come up with the idea of a new handbag boutique, but I'm only on Day 13 now and already feeling so confident about running my online store. I cannot wait to finally launch my store and cannot thank Denise enough for this great community and platform.

Roxine Grant

7 mins

Hi Everyone...new to the group but joined Run Boutique Members Club a few weeks ago. I have to say it's an amazing resource. I'm amazed by the level of expertise Denise has and is sharing for such an amazing price. Initially I didn't like that I couldn't see all of the info but I now love the step by step process and see the reason behind taking your time...this way you actually execute. It's perfect if you're building while working your full time job.

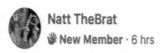

Natt TheBrat
✋ New Member · 6 hrs

I always wanted to learn how to have an online store. With being a fashion retail owner in the past, I didn't want to deal with the high overhead costs of today.

Run Boutique has shown me the way and with their step by step instructions , running my own store is turning into a reality.

Thank you for all the great knowledge you are passing onto new entrepreneurs everywhere. 💗

Tashieka Brown ▶ Start Online Boutique Members   •••
18 mins · 📷

Finding Run Boutique has been one of the best sites every. I am learning so much from this membership with the videos. It is teaching me the end and out, the highs and lows of starting a business. The information Ms.Denise gives, is so helpful. I would recommend anyone who doesn't have a clue on starting their online Boutique to definitely give it a try. You won't be disappointed.

WIN FREE ACCESS TO THE RUN BOUTIQUE BUSINESS KIT

As a thank you and bonus to you for purchasing and reading this book, I am pleased to also offer you the opportunity to WIN FREE Access to the Run Boutique Business Kit (worth thousands of dollars). To WIN access to this FREE kit, simply follow the 2 steps below;

1. Leave a Review of this Book on Amazon

2. Screenshot your review and email to

support@runboutique.com

A Discount Code will then be sent to you if you WIN for your **FREE Access to the Run Boutique Business Kit.**

*PLEASE NOTE: *Only verified purchase reviews will qualify.*

USEFUL RESOURCES

☐ Online Boutique Training Courses at:

www.runboutique.com

☐ Get business Cards and flyers at:

www.vistaprint.co.uk or www.vistaprint.com.

☐ Register a Domain Name at: **Namecheap**

☐ Get Web Hosting at: www.easyclickwebsites.com.

☐ Wholesale & Dropshipping Suppliers: Salehoo,

Worldwide Brands, Dropship Finds, Aliexpress

☐ Create an online store quickly at: Shopify

☐ Register Your Business at: https://www.irs.gov

(USA) or https://www.gov.uk (UK)

☐ To manage your day to day bookkeeping, you can

get this affordable bookkeeping software at

www.nohassleaccounting.com

REFERENCES

Craven, N. (2017, November 4). *Fashion website Missguided valued at £700m amid stock market float speculation.* Retrieved from This Is Money: http://www.thisismoney.co.uk/money/markets/article-5050057/700m-float-s-fashion-Missguided.html

Hamanaka, K. (2017, October 26). *PrettyLittleThing Parties With Kourtney Kardashian to Celebrate Collection.* Retrieved from WWD: http://wwd.com/eye/parties/prettylittlething-kourtney-kardashian-collection-11037000-11037000/

LaMonica, P. (2018, February 6). *Amazon worth more than Microsoft for first time.* Retrieved from CNN Money: http://money.cnn.com/2018/02/06/investing/amazon-microsoft-market-value/index.html

Nelson, E., & Karaian, J. (2018, April 10). *How much is Mark Zuckerberg worth?* Retrieved from QZ.COM: https://qz.com/1248927/what-is-mark-zuckerbergs-net-worth-in-2018/

Mintel. (2017, September 15). *BRITS HUNG UP ON ONLINE FASHION: ONLINE SALES OF CLOTHING, FASHION ACCESSORIES AND FOOTWEAR GROW BY 17% IN 2017.* Retrieved from Mintel Press: http://www.mintel.com/press-centre/fashion/uk-online-sales-of-clothing-fashion-accessories-and-footwear-grow-by-17-in-2017

PRNewswire. (2017, July 5). *The UK Clothing Market 2017-2022.*
Retrieved from PRNewswire:
https://www.prnewswire.com/news-releases/the-uk-
clothing-market-2017-2022-300483862.html

Winch, J. (2013, April 16). *8m Britons run online businesses from
home.* Retrieved from The Telegraph:
https://www.telegraph.co.uk/finance/personalfinance/
9997044/8m-Britons-run-online-businesses-from-
home.html

Williams-Grut, O. (2017, October 17). *ASOS sales pass £1.8
billion as profit jumps 145%.* Retrieved from Business
Insider UK: http://uk.businessinsider.com/asos-2017-
results-sales-profit-revenue-2017-10

Made in the USA
Columbia, SC
02 November 2021